A Guide To
Chesapeake

SEAFOOD DINING

BAYSIDE VIEWS
TO DINE BY

WHITEY SCHMIDT

MARIAN HARTNETT PRESS

CHESAPEAKE BAY REGIONS' MAP

Bayside Views
To Dine By

ILLUSTRATIONS BY
ROSEMARY HENRY-MAY

Printed in the
United States of America
First Printing 1988
ISBN 0-9613008-3-3

Library of Congress Catalog Number 88-80599
Copyright © 1988 by Marian Hartnett Press
Box 51, Friendship Road
Friendship, Maryland 20758

IV

CONTENTS

FEATURES

FEATURES

VII

INTRODUCTION

This book was written for people who love seafood or those who want to try a shore dinner or other regional specialty for the first time. The best place to find good seafood is, naturally, right on the coast where skipjacks, trawlers, and crab boats come in daily with fresh catches. This is particularly true of the Chesapeake Bay where restaurants share the shoreline. There is no better way to experience the full flavor of the Bay's history than to meander through the coastal towns, breathe the salt air, and steep yourself in the flavor of the past and a taste of today.

The waterfront restaurants profiled here represent a Bay sampler of those seafoods available. They include some of the best and some of the most obscure. Our format offers a brief note on each restaurant's house specialty, history, decor, and other features. It is not our intention to say that one kitchen's crab soup is better than another's, but to say that all have something that merits a try—whether a great view, terrific food, or a unique ambiance. In fact, nothing could be easier or quicker to serve than dishes that draw from nature's glorious bounty from the sea.

For the purpose of this book, we have divided the Bay area into 12 geographic regions. At times you may find yourselves looking out at a creek or a river, or perhaps a panoramic Bayside view. There is something for everyone— the excitement of major cities and the scenic calm of tiny and quiet backwaters. We leave the choice up to you.

Naturally, prices and hours of operation are subject to change. There are times when individual restaurants may suffer a shortage of supplies; therefore, it is a good idea to plan ahead and inquire by telephone. That way, you can be assured that you will have a seat by the window when you arrive.

Chesapeake cookery offers endless opportunities for exploration and delight. Chesapeake restaurants seem to have available an infinite variety of fish, clams, oysters, crabs, mussels, scallops and shrimp (sometimes supplemented by fresh or frozen seafood from faraway places), which is perfect for poaching, steaming, braising, stewing, baking, broiling, grilling, smoking, sauteing, stir frying, deep frying, or even raw on the half shell. Whether it be appetizers, soups, chowders, bisques, sandwiches, or entrees, seafood in general knows no culinary boundaries. So let the adventure begin.

MOVEABLE FEAST

Chesapeake Bay, Chesapeake free.
It's eating time for you and me.

You can have New York and all its glitter.
Give me the shore and an oyster fritter.

Just a walk out on a rickety pier,
Then sit by the window and drink a beer.

Harbor front road, Bay Creek back.
Catch a view of the lone skipjack.

The windows offer a relaxing mood.
so bring on the menu and bring on the food.

I don't want capers or liver pate,
Give me some crabs steamed in Old Bay.

Fresh baked biscuits topped with butter
That always make my tastebuds flutter.

Fresh shucked oysters, Smithfield hams,
Oyster Rockefeller, and casino clams.

Corn-on-the-cob and sliced tomatoes,
Fresh shore peaches, and home-fry taters.

Maryland crab soup, vegetable style,
And hot steamed oysters heaped in a pile.

So come by air, come by sloop,
Come and try the cream crab soup.

X

Come and try the fresh sea trout.
The good food is what it's all about.

You can drive around or sail across.
Bring the wife or bring the boss.

Come try what the good cook bakes.
Enjoy the taste of Virginia crab cakes.

Forget the Mac and quarter pounder.
Savor the taste of fresh baked flounder.

Fix your face, take a powder,
then try a bowl of fresh clam chowder.

She crab soup is hot and cheery.
Try a bowl topped with sherry.

Broiled blue fish makes a great filet.
Try some for dinner to brighten your day.

Watch for ducks up in the sky,
And look on the menu for oyster pie.

Chincoteague oysters with tabasco sauce,
Soft shell crabs are worth the cost.

You can charter a boat, round a crew,
Head on out for oyster stew.

Do they have steamed clams? Take a few.
Just get a table with a water view.

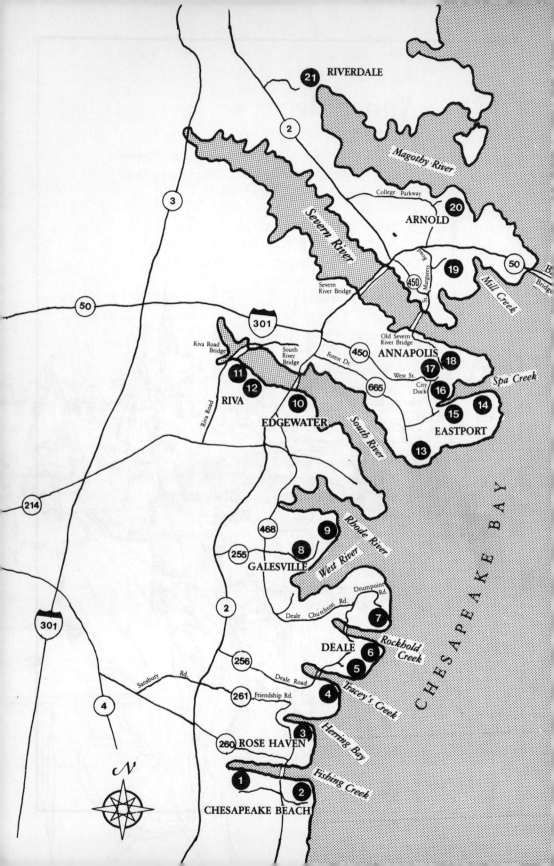

Annapolis
Waterfront Dining

INCLUDES: Chesapeake Beach, Rose Haven, Deale, Galesville, Edgewater, Riva, Annapolis, Arnold, and Riverdale, Maryland.

1. Abner's Seaside Crab House
2. Rod 'n' Reel Restaurant
3. Herrington Harbour Restaurant
4. Pierpoint Restaurant
5. Fisher's Wharf
6. Happy Harbor Inn
7. Skipper's Pier
8. Top Side Inn
9. The Inn at Pirate's Cove
10. The Crab Cafe
11. Paul's on the South River
12. Mike's Crab House
13. Dominique's
14. The Chart House
15. Carrol's Creek Cafe
16. Penthouse Wardroom Restaurant
17. Harbour House
18. Middleton Tavern
19. Jimmy Cantler's Riverside Inn
20. Deep Creek Restaurant
21. Riverdale Restaurant

ABNER'S SEASIDE CRAB HOUSE

Harbor Road
Chesapeake Beach, Maryland
301 / 257-3689

Business Season: all year

Hours: Sunday through Thursday—11 AM to 10 PM, Friday and Saturday—11 AM to 11 PM

Waterview: Fishing Creek / Chesapeake Bay

Credit Cards: MasterCard and Visa

House Specialties: cream of crab soup, clam chowder, oyster stew, clams on the half shell, oysters on the half shell, steamed crabs, crab cakes, soft shell crab, fried shrimp, steamed shrimp, stuffed shrimp, fried clams, fried oysters, stuffed hard crab, fresh catch of the day

The savory steamed blue crab found around the Chesapeake Bay is one of the most sought-after dishes by seafood lovers anywhere, and Abner's is a good place to get it. "Steaming the best since 1966," owner Bobby Abner features these crabs year round and specializes in other seafood delights as well. He's a professional waterman who also prepares his own daily catering for his customers.

For starters, there are always clams, oysters, and mussels by the dozen served steamed or raw, crab balls, barbecued shrimp, and a crab meat cocktail or steamed shrimp topped with Abner's special seasoning. For an entree, try Abner's Seafood Treat, a heaping platter of soft shell crabs, flounder, crab cake, fried clams, served with french fries and cole slaw. But I won't tell you any more. You must head on down to the Bay and try Abner's for yourself.

4

ROD 'N' REEL RESTAURANT

Bayside Road / Route 261
Chesapeake Beach, Maryland
301 / 257-2735

Business Season: all year except Christmas Day

Hours: open daily—11 AM to 10 PM

Waterview: Chesapeake Bay

Credit Cards: MasterCard and Visa

House Specialties: baked stuffed shrimp, broiled seafood platter, seafood Norfolk, mixed mariner's platter

The menu tells the Rod 'n' Reel's history.

"1898—Colorado railroad tycoons (led by Otto Mears) returned to the East to construct Washington's dream resort at Chesapeake Beach. This resort was to be equalled only by the French Riviera's Monte Carlo. The railroad began near the District line at Seat Pleasant and for years brought thousands here to Chesapeake Beach Park. Tourists also ventured from Baltimore on the Chesapeake by such steamboats as the 'Dreamland' and the 'J.S. Warden.'

"1930—The Park was moved from the boardwalk to the land, due to an ice storm.

"1933—Hurricane—The boardwalks, steamboat pier, roller coaster, and pavilions suffered serious damage.

"1948—Slot Machines were legalized in Southern Maryland, and business flourished.

"1965—The Restaurant business demanded more room, and two floors were added, the main dining room (first floor), and the Captain John Smith Room (Banquet Facilities, second floor). At this point, slot machines had 3 more years to go before the complete phase out that outlawed them.

"1983—Grand Opening of the Crab Deck, serving steamed crabs and spiced shrimp—in an outdoor setting—above the Charter Boats and harbor activity.

"NOW-We hope you enjoy the present as well as the past, our restaurant accommodations (everyday year 'round), banquet facilities, and charter fishing continue as ever popular spices to entice. The railroad station, and property on which it stands, was donated to the County by the Rod 'N' Reel Restaurant. The station has been restored to a museum and focal point for the preservation of our local heritage. We hope that you enjoy your visit here.''

HERRINGTON HARBOUR RESTAURANT

Route 261 (Lake Shore Drive)
Rose Haven, Maryland
301 / 741-5100

Business Season: all year

Hours: open daily—11 AM to 10 PM

Waterview: Herring Bay

Credit Cards: Visa, MasterCard, Choice

House Specialties: baked stuffed shrimp, catch of the day, fried flounder, broiled scallops, crab cakes, crab imperial, fried oysters, sauteed soft crabs, shrimp scampi, stuffed baked avocado, stuffed founder, cream of crab soup

You will enjoy reading the story the menu tells:
"In the beginning of the 17th century, Herring Bay was virtually unsettled and any trace of exploration is unknown. Spanish explorers are known to have arrived inside the Chesapeake Bay in 1566. Troubles with the Indians soon developed, which later caused discomfort for the English settlers. Here, peacefully but uneasily, the colonists lived with four major Indian tribes as their neighbors. Three of these tribes, the Piscataways of the Western Shore, and the Nanticokes and Pocomokes of the Eastern Shore, were of the larger Algonquin nation, all having similar dialects and customs. The Piscataways, of the Herrington Harbour area, also called the Conoys, comprised a number of smaller tribes that included: Mattawomans, Patuxents, Chopicans, Potopacs, Mattapanys, and Yaocomicoes. The other major tribe, the Susquehannocks (also known as the Conestoga), of the Iroquois nation, lived to the north of the Susquehanna River. As their settlements moved down the shores of the Chesapeake Bay, this warlike tribe of hunters often encountered and fought the Piscataways. The pressures from these tribes forced the Piscataways into a defensive alliance with the early colonists, enabling them to avoid serious clashes with other tribes.
"The Indians mode of life who lived in this area was basically the same as that of all northeast tribes. They built wigwams, round huts of bark over a framework of saplings, used shell money, made grooved stone axes and net-marked pottery. The Indians' fondness for oysters and clams is evident today by the numerous shells found in their refuse pits and large shell heaps along the shores. Hence, the name 'Chesapeake', which meant 'Great Shell Fish Bay', was born from these Indians. Recently, in 1977,

the Maryland Geological Survey conducted a dig, called the 'Rose Haven Site', on the grounds known as 'Chesapeake Overlook' , which is located several hundred yards north of Herrington Harbour. Most of the artifacts uncovered are now under study at the division of archaeology, Maryland Geological Survey Lab, in Baltimore. Additional artifacts are on exhibit in Merryman Hall at Johns Hopkins University. Items discovered locally include: soapstone bowls, grooved axes, arrowheads, and simple pottery. Interestingly, the results of the ongoing analysis suggest that the Rose Haven Site was occupied primarily during the summer months by small numbers of people who returned intermittently to approximately the same location during the time from about 400 A.D. to 900 A.D. . . .

" The first Englishman to visit this area of the Chesapeake Bay was Captain Lane, in 1585. He was accompanied by an artist, John White, who drew extremely accurate outline maps of the Chesapeake Bay and its tributaries and who later accompanied Sir Walter Raleigh's expeditions. Although he settled in Roanoke, N.C., records show that Sir Walter actually intended to settle on the shores of the Chesapeake Bay due to the influence of John White's maps. It is obvious that the Europeans were familiar with the Chesapeake Bay, and the Indians of this area were also familiar with the early settlers, before the English arrived at Jamestown. The first detailed records of settlers actually exploring these shores date from 1608, when Captain John Smith sailed the Chesapeake Bay. . . .

"In 1671, Quakers began holding quarterly meetings in a nearby settlement known as Herring Creek Hundred. Noted for their emphasis on education, the Quakers are believed to have built the first schoolhouse in Anne Arundel County at Herring Creek, which was later destroyed very early in the Civil War. Samuel Chew II, born at Herring Bay in 1660, was a Quaker and the grantor of the land on which Herring Creek Meeting House was built. He also started construction on the house known as "Maidstone" which was later completed in 1778. Legend has it that the ghost of his wife, Anne Ayres Chew dressed in gray with a long scarf blowing behind her, still walks in the garden in the evening. . . .

" . . . As time passed, the Herrington Harbour area, remained virtually unchanged until it was rediscovered in 1947 by Joseph Eugene Rose. It was his dream that was later to bloom into a beautiful flower for all to share as Herrington Harbour. To ensure that future generations do not lose sight of the beginning, and with some realization of what it took to create the past, we dedicate this menu to you, our guest."

Herrington Harbour Restaurant is situated on the waters edge overlooking the largest marina on the Chesapeake Bay.

PIERPOINT RESTAURANT
420 Deale Road
Deale, Maryland
301 / 867-1225

Business Season: March to December

Hours: Wednesday—5 PM to 10 PM, Thursday through Saturday— 11 AM to 11 PM, Monday and Tuesday—closed

Waterview: Tracy's Creek / Herring Bay

Credit Cards: Visa, MasterCard, Choice

House Specialties: broiled stuffed flounder, fried seafood sampler, broiled seafood platter, soft shell crabs, broiled or fried scallops, crab cakes

The menu reads:

"Legend has it that in the early 17th century a ship was caught in a violent storm off the Chesapeake Bay. The rig went down, but the captain and crew survived by floating on wooden planks. And the captain, clutching a treasure of family heirloom recipes, floated all the way to a pier on Tracy Creek in Deale, Maryland. At the exact point where he came ashore now sits the Pierpoint Restaurant. You may not believe the legend, but the truth is, you're about to savor the finest specialties of your host owner, Chef Tanios. Chef Tanios has over 5 years of cooking with love from his early training in London to his past 15 years as well-known caterer to celebrities, public figures, embassies and members of the Senate and Congress in the Nation's Capital. He invites you to share the pleasure that cooking with passion creates!"

FISHER'S WHARF

477 Deale Road
Deale, Maryland
301 / 867-0511

Business Season: year around

Hours: Monday through Thursday—11 AM to 11 PM, Friday and Saturday—11 AM to 2 AM, Sunday—11 AM to midnight

Waterview: Rockhold Creek / Herring Bay

Credit Cards: none

House Specialties: steamed crabs, crab cakes, soft shell crab sandwich, oysters

Fisher's Wharf is a pine-panelled waterman's bar that was built around 1940. Not much has changed since then except the owners. As you travel down Rockhold Creek Drive, look for the large new sign that displays the menu.

Once inside you will have no trouble making a selection for the entire menu could be printed on a 3 x 5 card. Check with your server and order what's hot. The cook does an outstanding job with the crabs. I love to visit here when looking for a bushel of oysters to carry home.

HAPPY HARBOR INN
533 Deale Road
Deale, Maryland
301 / 867-0949

Business Season: all year

Hours: open daily—7 AM to 2 AM

Waterview: Rockhold Creek / Herring Bay

Credit Cards: Visa, MasterCard, Choice

House Specialties: cream of crab soup, imperial stuffed soft shell crabs, steamed clams, fried clams, crab cakes, steamed crabs, fried fish

Travel north up the Bay, and you will eventually reach Deale, a tiny waterman's community. This town offers many marine facilities that are clustered around a small bridge. Deale is also home to the Happy Harbor Inn, where boaters, bikers, and bird watchers gather. I like to visit here to feast on homemade crab cakes on a bun or crackers, with a dash of hot sauce.

The Happy Harbor regularly features several seafood dinners—crab Norfolk, stuffed shrimp, and broiled scallops. In addition, each night of the week a different special is offered: on Monday, prime rib; Tuesday—buffet or fish fry; Wednesday—crab; Friday—clams; Saturday—shrimp sampler platter; and Sunday—imperial stuffed soft shell crabs.

SKIPPER'S PIER
6158 Drum Point Road
Deale, Maryland
301 / 867-7110

Business Season: April to November

Hours: St. Patrick's Day through Memorial Day—limited hours, Memorial Day through Labor Day open daily—10 AM to 11 PM

Waterview: Rockhold Creek / Herring Bay

Credit Cards: Visa and MasterCard

House Specialties: fresh steamed crabs, steamed maninose, beer-batter fried flounder, crab cakes, soft shell crabs, seafood platter, fried oyster sandwich, steamed oysters, oysters on the half shell

Your hosts, Sherry and John B., are looking forward to another season with their friends at the end of Drum Point Road in beautiful Deale, Maryland. A friendly home-away-from-home, Skipper's Pier offers an elevated deck with a Chesapeake Bay view. If you're there in August, steamed crabs are half price on Wednesdays. Or time your visit to watch the blue crabs going through the shedding process at the pier.

Several fishing charters are available aboard the "Miss Concrete III." From our seats on the outdoor deck we watched the ship returning from a day of fishing on the Bay. We looked around to see a large cockatoo in a cage shaded from the sun. We also watched the fireboat parked at the pier with its bright red letters and large red pumps.

The large blackboard menu read, "The Queen Is In." We learned that this meant that the local favorite, "Silver Queen Corn," was freshly picked, prepared and ready for eatin'. Yum!

TOP SIDE INN

Riverside Drive
Galesville, Maryland
301 / 867-1321

Business Season: all year

Hours: Monday through Friday—4 PM to 10:30 PM, Saturday and Sunday—7 AM to 10:30 PM

Waterview: West River

Credit Cards: Visa, MasterCard, American Express, Choice

House Specialties: soft shell crab almondine, crab cake, fried oyster, broiled flounder, sauteed scallops, fried shrimp

The Top Side Inn offers three delightful homemade soups with which to begin your meal—vegetable crab, cream of crab, or clam chowder. Then you can choose from the list of appetizers. I particularly liked the oyster on the half shell, jumbo shrimp cocktail, and crab ball cocktail.

Dinner choices include nine seafood entrees in addition to various beef, fowl, and Italian dishes. I chose the soft shell crab almondine. Sauteed in creamy butter to a crisp brown, these crabs were a mouth-watering delight. You might try the fried oysters, lightly breaded and fried to a rich, even brown. They are not only delicious but nutritious as well. All entrees are served with garden salad, potato, and bread with butter.

THE INN AT PIRATE'S COVE

Riverside Drive
Galesville, Maryland
301 / 867-2300

Business Season: all year

Hours: Sunday through Thursday—lunch from 11 AM, dinner 5 PM to 10 PM, Friday and Saturday—11 AM to 10 PM

Waterview: West River

Credit Cards: Visa, MasterCard, American Express

House Specialties: broiled shellfish platter (lobster tail, shrimp, scallops, and clams casino) cream of crab soup, crab cakes, crab imperial

History tells us that back in the 1600's and early 1700's, pirates, buccaneers, and corsairs roamed up and down the Atlantic coastline raiding the many vessels from Europe which were pouring into the New World. Many pirates used the sheltered bays and inlets of Maryland's western shore and Chesapeake Bay to hide out, refit their battle-damaged ships, and sometimes, to bury treasure. One of the many thousands of bars, islands, or secluded headlands could easily still be holding a fortune buried beneath its sand by Blackbeard or one of his peers.

If, like the crew aboard Blackbeard's vessel, you are seeking treasure, then claim this fine seafood restaurant as your bounty. Its commitment to freshness means that seafood selections are dictated by market and seasonal availability. Ask your waiter for the day's choices. I especially like the twin lobster tail, shrimp, clams, or mussels steamed in sauce marinara on a bed of linguini.

You may ask to have your selection broiled with herb butter, poached in court bouillon, sauteed in sweet butter, or deep fried. All entrees are served with fresh-baked bread, still warm from the oven, with butter, garden salad, potato, and vegetables.

Appetizers from the oyster bar include four cold, three steamed, and eight hot dishes from the oven. And if you still have room after dinner, try one of 14 intriguing international coffees.

THE CRAB CAFE
48 South River Road
Edgewater, Maryland
301 / 956-5006
301 / 269-6838

Business Season: March to December

Hours: open daily—11 AM to 11 PM

Waterview: South River

Credit Cards: MasterCard, Visa, American Express

House Specialties: steamed crabs, stuffed shrimp, fried shrimp, crab imperial, crab cakes, soft crab platter

It was early spring when I visited the Crab Cafe at the Pier 7 Marina. We entered through a glassed-in outdoor porch. A bar and large room were formed by a series of sliding panels. There was a stone fireplace. The room was filled with plants, and a pet parrot squawked continuously as we passed through to the outdoor deck high above the manicured lawn and boat yard.

Sitting down, we glanced around to view a party of six unloading from a power boat at the pier. The dockside patio filled quickly with patrons enjoying the lovely day. The view of the South River was breathtaking. There was a light southerly wind and not a cloud in the sky. The blackboard menu listed the specials of the day: catfish Cajun style, deep-fried crab cakes, and cream of broccoli soup.

PAUL'S ON THE SOUTH RIVER

3027 Riva Road
Riva, Maryland
301 / 956-3410

Business Season: all year

Hours: lunch—Tuesday through Friday 11:30 AM to 3 PM, dinner—Tuesday through Sunday 5 PM to 10 PM, closed Monday

Waterview: South River

Credit Cards: MasterCard, Visa, American Express, Choice, Diners Club

House Specialties: catch of the day, shrimp scampi, soft shell clams, oysters on the half shell, crab cakes, soft crabs, combination seafood platter, crab imperial, stuffed shrimp, stuffed flounder imperial, cream of crab soup, seafood bisque, seafood salad

Paul's offers the seafood lover one of the finest menus on the Chesapeake Bay's western shore. The food is not only skillfully prepared, but served with style. Take, for example, the "seafood array," a seasoned saute of any six of the following—petite lobster tail, jumbo gulf shrimp, Canadian scallops, Boston swordfish, Maine mussels, Norwegian salmon, flounder filet, backfin crab cake, and shucked Chincoteague oysters. Or consider as a romantic dinner for two: the lobster 'n' loin—twin stuffed whole Maine lobsters steamed and served with tender cuts of filet mignon char-grilled to your liking. Another excellent dish is chateaubriand—broiled center-cut of whole tenderloin with bouquetiere of fresh vegetables and bearnaise sauce. The waiter will carve the meat at your table. I could go on.

If you visit Paul's, you won't be disappointed. Reservations are requested.

MIKE'S CRAB HOUSE

3030 Riva Road
Riva, Maryland
301 / 956-2784

Business Season: all year

Hours: Monday through Friday—11 AM to 10 PM, Saturday and Sunday—11 AM to 11 PM

Waterview: South River

Credit Cards: Visa, MasterCard, American Express

House Specialties: crab imperial, seafood combination, crab cakes, fried shrimp, broiled scallops, fried scallops

Located on the beautiful South River, Mike's Crab House is a wonderful spot to stop for a while. Pay a visit to the large bar or the spacious adjoining restaurant that offers an extensive selection of seafood and beef for moderate prices.

Begin your dinner with an appetizer—king crab legs, rock shrimp, Greek salad, oysters on the half shell, crab soup, or a bucket of soft shell clams steamed to perfection. Then choose from among 15 seafood entries, 4 beef dishes, fried chicken, or stuffed grape leaves. An excellent choice is the crab house special—stuffed hard crab with french fries and coleslaw. The dessert menu, however, is somewhat limited, offering only cheese cake and ice cream.

If the weather is right, enjoy your meals outside, flanked by the prettiest canna lillies you will ever see. You'll have a view of both the Riva Road Bridge and the new South River Bridge. And you'll see pleasure craft on the river, plenty of them, both power and sail.

DOMINIQUE'S
2020 Chesapeake Harbour Drive
Annapolis, Maryland
301 / 263-3600

Business Season: all year

Hours: Monday through Thursday—1:30 AM to midnight, Friday and Saturday—11:30 AM to 1 AM, Sunday—10 AM to 9 PM

Waterview: Chesapeake Harbour / Chesapeake Bay

Credit Cards: MasterCard, Visa, American Express

House Specialties: oysters and clams on the half shell, grilled salmon, steamed mussels, grilled swordfish, crab meat casserole, stuffed shrimp, soft shell crabs

At Dominique's, the atmosphere is a fine balance of casualness and class in a brand new building built to look like a lighthouse from the early 1900's. The challenge for owner Dominique D'Ermo was to create a restaurant that is both elegant yet casual enough to be comfortable for boaters wearing deck shoes.

The first floor has seating for about 85. It includes a glass-enclosed sun room that overlooks the marina and an outside deck. Upstairs in Sam's Retreat Lounge, patrons sitting at the bar also have a view of the marina.

The more exotic dishes have helped to make D'Ermo's restaurants in Washington, D.C., and Miami, Florida, successful. Now, I didn't try the Florida alligator or the Texas rattlesnake, but I did try the crab cake and was rewarded with a classic version of this regional delicacy. It's hard to go wrong with anything you order, and the service is excellent, prompt, and not over-intrusive. Will I see you there?

THE CHART HOUSE

300 Second Street
Annapolis, Maryland
301 / 268-7166

Business Season: all year

Hours: open daily—Monday through Thursday—5 PM to 10 PM, Friday and Saturday—5 PM to 11 PM, Sunday brunch—11 AM to 2 PM, Sunday dinner—4 PM to 10 PM

Waterview: Spa Creek / Severn River

Credit Cards: American Express, MasterCard, Visa, Diners Club

House Specialties: cream of crab soup, fresh fish, clam chowder, broiled scallops, crab imperial, stuffed flounder, crab cakes

Eastport is a peninsula with stores and facilities committed to locals and boaters. Main supply businesses, snug anchorages, and shipyards were built on Spa Creek as early as 1650. Once a small village of cottages and boatyards, Eastport now has high-rise apartment buildings.

The tiny streets with their nautical charm are worth exploring. One of their treasures is the Chart House, where the decor takes you back in time to when sailmakers performed their craft in historic Annapolis.

This restaurant and lounge overlooking Annapolis Harbor specializes in steaks, seafood, and an extensive salad bar. It's always busy, so plan to arrive early. The quality of the food is matched by the impeccable service.

CARROL'S CREEK CAFE
410 Severn Avenue
Annapolis, Maryland
301 / 263-8102

Business Season: all year

Hours: lunch—11 AM to 4 PM, dinner—from 5 PM, Sunday brunch—11 AM to 3 PM, Sunday dinner—5 PM to 10 PM

Waterview: Spa Creek

Credit Cards: Visa, MasterCard, American Express

House Specialties: crab meat Remick, barbecued shrimp, gumbo, catfish, trout, cream of crab soup, oysters on the half shell, clams casino, crab salad, crab imperial, soft shell crabs

From the kitchen of Carrol's Creek Cafe comes a new American tradition of food—blackened fish (K-Paul's style), Texas style barbecued shrimp and bacon accompanied by a warm cucumber salad; baked fresh flounder; Cape Cod sea scallops sauteed with garlic, basil, and cream; or boneless breast of chicken stuffed with fresh spinach and sausage and topped with mornay sauce. If you're feeling adventurous, try the buffalo tenderloin topped with "Little Big Horn Sauce." At my last visit, I feasted on savory soft shell crabs washed down by plenty of cold Bass Ale.

If you like Sunday brunch, then try Carrol's. The *Baltimore Magazine* declared it to be one of Maryland's best.

But food is not the only attraction. The Cafe overlooks Spa Creek, offering patrons a spectacular view of hundreds of sailboats. This mid-town waterfront area is the hub of colonial Annapolis with its yachting facilities and charter services. It is also the location of national attractions such as art festivals and sailboat and powerboat shows.

Carrol's says, "The use of fine, fresh, uniquely American products is the basis of our cooking." I think you will agree.

PENTHOUSE WARDROOM RESTAURANT

80 Compromise Street
Annapolis, Maryland
301 / 268-7555

Business Season: all year

Hours: open daily—7 AM to 11 PM

Waterview: Spa Creek / Severn River

Credit Cards: MasterCard, Visa, American Express, Diners Club

House Specialties: steamed clams, mussels in garlic sauce, crab meat cocktail, oysters on the half shell, clams on the half shell, blackened red fish, barbequed swordfish, shrimp stuffed with crab meat, seafood Norfolk, crab cakes, imperial crab, soft shell crabs

Annapolis is located midway between Baltimore, Maryland, and Washington, D.C. As a port-of-entry it is ideally situated, being 2 miles from the Chesapeake Bay on the south bank of the Severn River. The Penthouse Wardroom Restaurant, located on the fifth floor of the Annapolis Hilton, has one of the outstanding waterfront views the Bay has to offer. From your seat high above the harbor, you can watch passengers board the "Harbor Queen," one of several tour boats that ply the harbor and creeks of Annapolis. Or, perhaps you'll spot the "jiffy taxi" that picks up passengers from their boats and delivers them to their dockside destination.

The day I visited, the crab cakes were as "big as your fist" and filled with large, sweet chunks of crab. They were accompanied by large fries, tartar sauce, cocktail sauce, and ketchup. The open dark-wood room was complete with red chairs and carpet. The tables had plain white tablecloths, and a fresh red carnation adorned each. The constant boat traffic and a view of America's only 18th century waterfront combined to make my visit a success.

HARBOUR HOUSE

87 Prince George Street
Annapolis, Maryland
301 / 268-0771

Business Season: all year

Hours: open daily—11:30 AM to 10 PM

Waterview: Spa Creek / Severn River

Credit Cards: American Express, MasterCard, Visa

House Specialties: crab cakes, crab quiche, fried oyster sandwich, clams on the half shell, seafood pie, bouillabaisse, crab imperial, fisherman's platter, stuffed shrimp, oysters on the half shell, oysters Rockefeller, cream of crab soup, clam chowder

The menu story states:
"George Phillips captured the waterfront flavor of Annapolis when he came to town in 1960 and opened his small restaurant on the part of the City Dock known to locals as 'Hell Point,' the home of watermen for 300 years. Baltimore-born and Marriott-trained, George Phillips had the vision to see the City Dock reviving as a place of commerce in the midst of burgeoning Annapolis. His original 90-seat restaurant—with George, himself preparing steaks and seafood on an open broiler 'beneath the gleaming cooper hood' became the town's most popular dining spot.

"Over the past decades, George Phillips' Harbour House has not only grown in size—to 390 seats—but has become an Annapolis landmark and a Maryland dining tradition, known for sensational seafood, steaks and prime rib.

"The original Harbour House, located on the first floor, has been redesigned into an elegant, contemporary room—called Brendan's Room, used for dining and special functions.

"In addition, George and his sons, Glenn and Kurt, operate The Terrace, an outdoor dining deck adjacent to the Harbour House. The Terrace evokes the mood of the open air cafes of Europe. Open May through October, The Terrace offers a combination of finger foods, soups, salads, sandwiches and unique features."

George Phillips invites you to enjoy the great choice of dining at his restaurants on the City Dock.

MIDDLETON TAVERN

2 Market-Space
Annapolis, Maryland
301 / 263-3323

Business Season: all year

Hours: open daily—11:30 AM to 10 PM, Sunday brunch—10 AM to 2:30 PM

Waterview: Spa Creek / Severn River

Credit Cards: MasterCard and Visa

House Specialties: oysters on the half shell, clams on the half shell, steamed oysters, steamed mussels, smoked blue fish, crab cocktail, crab soup, crab imperial, catch of the day, crab cakes, seafood crepes

Established in 1750, Middleton Tavern was once host to a galaxy of prominent patrons including George Washington, Thomas Jefferson, and Benjamin Franklin. Today, dine there yourself and enjoy the authentic colonial fireside setting or the outdoor cafe, which overlooks the city dock in Olde Annapolis Towne.

JIMMY CANTLER'S RIVERSIDE INN

458 Forest Beach Road
Annapolis, Maryland
301 / 757-1311

Business Season: all year

Hours: Sunday through Thursday—10 AM to 11 PM, Friday and Saturday—10 AM to midnight

Waterview: Mill Creek / Severn River

Credit Cards: none

House Specialties: steamed clams, steamed crabs, catch of the day, seafood platter, soft shell crabs, crab imperial, crab cakes

You can't pass Jimmy Cantler's Riverside Inn by accident, because it's at the end of a dead-end road overlooking Mill Creek. To get there, take Route 50 east to the Howard Johnsons, then turn right onto Old Mill Road. Turn right again onto St. Margaret's Road, go 2 miles, U-turn at Sandy's Country Store, and take the next right onto Forest Beach Road. Once you reach the Inn, you may not want to leave, for the food is among the freshest that you will find anywhere.

The Riverside Inn has become an institution over the years for its delicious steamed clams, shrimp, and crabs. Listen to this schedule of specialties: Monday—steamed clams; Tuesday—shrimp salad, steamed shrimp and steamed oysters; Thursday—soft crab; and Friday—the catch of the day, always freshly caught and cooked by a member of the Cantler family.

DEEP CREEK RESTAURANT

1058 Deep Creek Avenue
Arnold, Maryland
301 / 757-4045

Business Season: all year

Hours: open daily—11:30 AM to 10 PM

Waterview: Deep Creek / Magothy River

Credit Cards: American Express, Visa, MasterCard

House Specialties: oysters Rockefeller, oysters casino, oysters barbequed, beer-batter fried shrimp, crab cakes, crab imperial, bouillabaisse, fish sampler, baked scallops

Every winter this area of the Bay is home to some of the Maryland Skipjack Fleet, the only sail-powered workboat fleet remaining in the United States. The crew aboard offers visitors a rare view of 19th century-style workboats. Law prohibits the dredging of oysters using power boats in public beds, so these workboats are able to provide a valuable service.

It's best to call for directions and reservations at the newly renovated Deep Creed Restaurant and raw bar located on the Magothy River. Check the blackboard menu for the day's dinner specials. On Monday and Tuesday it's bouillabaisse crammed full of seafood delights. On Wednesday and Thursday, it's a fresh fish sampler with three varieties of fresh fish served with two vegetables. All entrees are served with your choice of two house salads, fresh vegetable of the day, baked stuffed potato, or curley fries.

A house favorite I enjoy is the beer-batter fried shrimp. Scallops Monterey is another house special that brings raves. Here, fresh scallops are baked in a mild cheese sauce with fresh tomatoes, mushrooms, and scallions. The broiled oyster sampler is also outstanding.

RIVERDALE RESTAURANT

143 Inverness Road
Riverdale, Maryland
301 / 647-9830

Business Season: all year

Hours: open daily—12 noon to 2 AM

Waterview: Magothy River

Credit Cards: Visa and MasterCard

House Specialties: crab soup, crab cake, imperial crab, fried shrimp, crab salad, shrimp salad, crab meat cocktail, combination platter, fried scallops, lobster tail stuffed with crab imperial

At the Riverdale Restaurant delicious food, informal surroundings, and a scenic view of the Magothy River combine to provide an interlude of relaxing dining. Owners Charlie and Dee Vane say, "May we suggest you enjoy your favorite drink while we prepare your meal with all the loving care of authentic home cooking."
We suggest you give them a try.

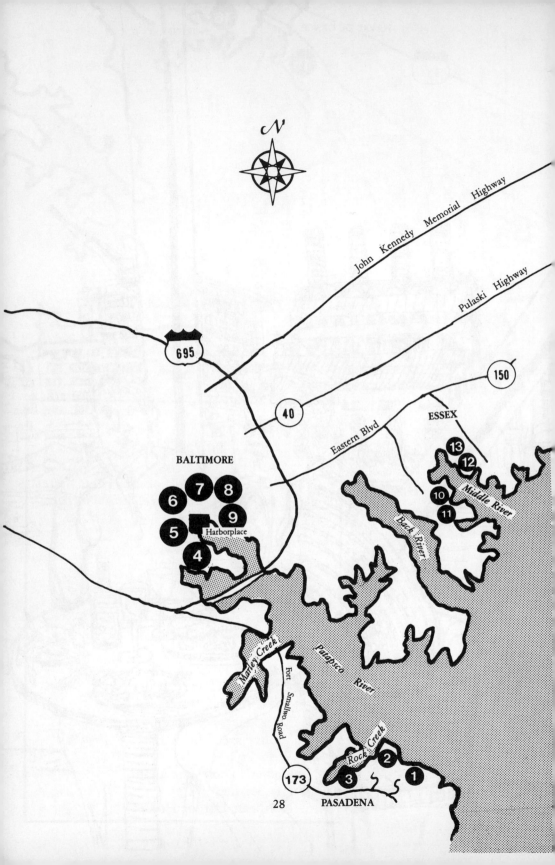

Map labels:

HAVRE DE GRACE

NORTHEAST

95

16

15

Susquehanna River

Northeast River

ABERDEEN

Perryman Road

C H E S A P E A K E   B A Y

Bush River

14

Baltimore
Waterfront Dining

INCLUDES: Pasadena, Baltimore, Essex, Aberdeen, Havre de Grace, and Northeast, Maryland.

1. Antonio's on the Bay
2. The Galley Restaurant
3. The Oak Point Inn
4. Rusty Scupper
5. Phillips Harbor Place
6. The American Cafe
7. City Lights
8. Mariner's Pier One
9. The Chart House
10. The Driftwood Inn
11. River watch Restaurant
12. Whitey and Dot's
13. Wilhelm's
14. Gabler's Shore Restaurant
15. Bay Steamer
16. Northeast Harbor House

ANTONIO'S ON THE BAY

2042 Knoll View Drive
Pasadena, Maryland
301 / 437-4445

Business Season: all year

Hours: open daily—11:30 AM to 10 PM

Waterview: Chesapeake Bay

Credit Cards: American Express, Visa, Choice, Diners Club, MasterCard

House Specialties: baked crab imperial, surf and turf, seafood combination platter, crab cakes, fried shrimp, broiled scallops, fried scallops, oysters on the half shell

Antonio's provides you with a breathtaking view of the Chesapeake Bay looking out towards Baltimore and some good seafood too. But it's worth going there just for a drink. Here are just a few:

Pina Coladas:

Almond	Amaretto	Apple
Apricot	Banana	Blue Curcao
Blackberry	Cherry	Chocolate Mint
Chocolate	Chocolate Cherry	Coffee
Cinnamon	Comfort	Kahlua
Licorice	Lime	Mocha
Melon	Mint	Raspberry
Orange	Ouzo	Rum
Peach	Peppermint	Spearmint
Strawberry	Swiss Choc Almond	Wild Cherry
Toasted Almond	Vanilla	

The following around-the-world coffees:

Antonio's: amaretto, brandy, coffee topped with whipped cream, stemmed cherry, and kahlua

Jamaican: Tia Maria, syrup, coffee topped with whipped cream, stemmed cherry, and kahlua

French: cognac, green creme de menthe syrup, coffee topped with whipped cream, stemmed cherry, and kahlua

THE GALLEY RESTAURANT
White Rocks Yachting Center
1402 Colony Road
Pasadena, Maryland
301 / 255-4424

Business Season: all year

Hours: open daily—11:30 AM to 2:30 PM

Waterview: Rock Creek / Patapsco River

Credit Cards: MasterCard and Visa

House Specialties: crab soup, spiced shrimp, seafood platter, lobster tail stuffed with crab meat, broiled scallops, crab cakes, crab imperial, shrimp scampi, shrimp imperial, seafood Newburg, sole almondine, fried oysters

This restaurant may well be Rock Creek's best kept secret. It is a delightful spot for enjoying either casual, light fare or elegant, full course, fireside dining. If you find it crowded inside, try The Galley's waterside patio deck and enjoy the sight of many sailboats.

Begin your meal with mouth watering Maryland crab soup, vegetable style, or spiced shrimp steamed to your order. Leading the way on a menu that offers 18 entrees are the lobster tails, succulent treats broiled to perfection. If crab imperial is your choice, take note that this delicate lump of crab is laced with an imperial mixture and topped with the chef's imperial glaze. Another excellent choice is oysters Chesapeake, world famous Chincoteague oysters deep fried in a delicate bread coating to a golden brown. All entrees are served with salad, baked potato, and hot rolls with butter.

The management says, "We are more than just another sleepy little marina restaurant." So why not enjoy the Galley's comfortable atmosphere and gracious hospitality?

THE OAK POINT INN
7617 Water Oak Point Road
Pasadena, Maryland
301 / 437-7221

Business Season: all year

Hours: 11 AM to 11 PM, closed Mondays

Waterview: Rock Creek / Magothy River

Credit Cards: Visa, MasterCard, American Express

House Specialties: broiled seafood platter, fried seafood platter, crab soup, crab cakes, crab bisque, oysters on the half shell, catch of the day, crab imperial, crab cakes, stuffed shrimp, sauteed scallops

It was early spring on a gusty day, when I discovered the Oak Point Inn. The wind moved the clouds above, and the restaurant was well staffed as they were planning the season's rush when boats and seafood lovers flock to the area.

When you want a simple lunch, quickly acquired, but you seek a homemade quality as well, the Oak Point Inn is just about right. The menu is simple. Appetizers are many. For example, you can order oysters, 6 on the half shell, 12 on the half shell, Rockefeller, or fried. Clams are served four ways, and a hot sampler that brought raves consisted of clams, oysters, shrimp cocktail, and crab claws.

Seafood entrees are served with fresh baked bread and butter, choice of spinach or tossed salad, choice of baked potato or rice, and vegetable du jour. Entrees include broiled flounder, grilled swordfish, and catch of the day. The menu states, "If, for any reason you would prefer your meal prepared differently than our normal method, please do not hesitate to ask your server. We will do our best to accommodate your special needs."

RUSTY SCUPPER
402 Key Highway
Baltimore, Maryland
301 / 727-3678

Business Season: all year, closed Christmas Day

Hours: Monday through Saturday—lunch 11 AM to 2:30 PM,
Monday through Thursday—dinner 5 PM to 10 PM, Friday and
Saturday—dinner 5 PM to 11 PM, Sunday— 1 PM to 9 PM

Waterview: Inner Harbor / Patapsco River

Credit Cards: American Express, MasterCard, Visa, Diners Club,
Carte Blanche

House Specialties: shrimp teriyaki, barbecued shrimp, shrimp
linguini, clam chowder, shrimp cocktail, smoked trout, catch of
the day, shrimp and vegetable stir fry, soft shell crab sandwich

What is a "scupper?" Well, it's California slang for a tugboat that's
used to ply the waters of the San Francisco Bay. And the California look
is carried over inside this multileveled restaurant whose generous portions
are an important aspect of this San Francisco-based chain. There's lots of
greenery and lots of glass.

Part of Baltimore's famous Inner Harbor Marina, the restaurant is
located opposite the National Aquarium. There are many levels from which
you can enjoy the view from the outer deck, and you can view the U.S.S.
Trenton from Norfolk, Virginia.

PHILLIPS HARBORPLACE
301 Light Street
Baltimore, Maryland
301 / 685-6600

Business Season: all year

Hours: open daily—11 AM to 11 PM

Waterview: Inner Harbor / Patapsco River

Credit Cards: MasterCard, Visa, Choice, American Express, Diners Club

House Specialties: crab cakes, crab imperial, steamed shrimp, oysters on the half shell, clam bake, seafood platter, crab imperial, fish of the day

Phillips serves fresh fish broiled, baked, or fried. The menu offers the following information about two popular selections:

"Seatrout
Seatrout is also known by its coastal Indian name Squeateague, Weakfish, and Summer Trout. An important gamefish on the Eastern Shore, it deserves three stars at table. Primarily a surf fish, Seatrout begin to show around the Chesapeake and Delaware Bays in April. Seatrout then spread in great numbers along the coast to New England, The flesh of the Seatrout is sweet, white, lean, and firmly textured.

"Swordfish
Swordfish are found throughout the world in tropical and temperate seas, and in the western Atlantic are taken from Newfoundland to Cuba. They are present off our coast usually from late June through the summer, then move offshore into deep water along the edge of the Continental Shelf. Everywhere it occurs the swordfish is greatly esteemed and brings top prices at market. Swordfish has a rich, mild flavor and a firm, dense, meat-like texture which lends itself perfectly to grilling."

THE AMERICAN CAFE
301 Light Street
Baltimore, Maryland
301 / 962-8800

Business Season: all year

Hours: Monday through Thursday—11 AM to 1 AM, Friday through Sunday—11 AM to 2 AM

Waterview: Inner Harbor / Patapsco River

Credit Cards: MasterCard, Visa, American Express, Diners Club, Choice

House Specialties: crayfish bisque, lobster and scallop pie, shrimp and crab meat pizza, crab cakes, grilled bluefish, grilled red-fish, crab salad, catch of the day

Light but elegant cuisine is the specialty here, featuring regional American entrees, homemade salads, sandwiches, and desserts. Here is a sampling from the dinner menu;
Black Bean Soup Garnished with Sour Cream and
    Diced Red Peppers
Spinach Salad with Warm Zinfandel Dressing
Fresh Center-Cut Tuna Steak Wrapped in Cabbage
Mandoline Vegetables
Cornbread Sticks
Chocolate Amaretto Pate with Toasted Almonds
    and Raspberry Puree

CITY LIGHTS

301 Light Street
Baltimore, Maryland
301 / 244-8811

Business Season: all year

Hours: open daily—lunch 11:30 AM to 3:30 PM, dinner—5 PM to 10:30 PM

Waterview: Inner Harbor / Patapsco River

Credit Cards: American Express, Visa, MasterCard, Choice, Diners Club, Carte Blanche

House Specialties: fried oysters, crab cakes, steamed shrimp, crab soup, clams on the half shell, oysters on the half shell, shrimp scampi, steamed seafood platter, crab meat and scallop casserole

During the warm summer evenings, City Lights retracts its side walls, turning the establishment into a sidewalk cafe. A special treat here is the coffee—Irish, West Coast, East Coast, Spanish, or the house specialty. City Lights' spicy version of a Maryland tradition, crab soup, is chock full of hunks of crab. I followed it with the specialty of the day, shrimp scampi, which was delicious.

Afterwards, if you like boats, don't pass up a tour of the U.S.F. Constellation, which is birthed just outside the restaurant. This ship was first launched in Baltimore on September 7, 1797. In 1799, it became the first commissioned ship of the U.S. Navy. The Constellation also served in the War of 1812, the Civil War, and as flag ship in World War II.

MARINER'S PIER ONE

201 East Pratt Street
Baltimore, Maryland
301 / 962-5050

Business Season: all year

Hours: open daily—11:30 AM to 10 PM

Waterview: Inner Harbor / Patapsco River

Credit Cards: Visa, MasterCard, Choice, American Express, Diners Club, Carte Blanche

House Specialties: shrimp cocktail, clam chowder, clams casino, crab soup, fish of the day, crab cakes, shrimp scampi, broiled scallops, fried breaded shrimp, shrimp salad, fresh flounder, oyster bake

On one rainy day, I sat in this street-level restaurant looking out upon the beautiful Baltimore Harborplace. The view was so good that it was like being inside and outside at the same time. My selection, fresh flounder, was broiled with a hint of lemon and rich creamy butter. The price was reasonable.

You might wish to begin with Mariner's oyster bake. In this dish, Chesapeake oysters are baked on the half shell in a creamy white sauce with shrimp and mushrooms and crowned with mozzarella cheese. The Mariner's Seafood Bounty was a dish we especially enjoyed. It consisted of a medley of backfin crab balls, scallops, batter-dipped oysters, and shrimp.

THE CHART HOUSE

601 East Pratt Street
Baltimore, Maryland
301 / 539-6616

Business Season: all year

Hours: open daily—11:30 AM to 10:30 PM

Waterview: Inner Harbor / Patapsco River

Credit Cards: Visa and MasterCard

House Specialties: cream of crab soup, oysters Rockefeller, oysters casino, fresh fish of the day, broiled scallops, crab cakes, soft shell crab, baked stuffed flounder, clam chowder, shrimp cocktail

The National Aquarium is a place you must visit when at the Inner Harbor. Then walk across the pedestrian bridge and sample the bounty that the Chart House has to offer. It is located in an old warehouse that has been renovated into a light-filled and airy restaurant. You can choose to eat on an outdoor patio or in the two-story, glass-topped building with ceilings containing large beams.

One good reason for visiting the Chart House is the seafood bar, where selections include oysters on the half shell, oysters or clams casino, clams or oysters Rockefeller, clams on the half shell, Maryland cream of crab soup, New England clam chowder, shrimp cocktail, spiced shrimp, and baked brie with sliced almonds. I selected oysters on the half shell and Maryland cream of crab soup and was rewarded with a superb meal.

The menu also lists a "super deli sandwich." Choose from crab salad, roast beef, smoked ham, or smoked turkey with bread and cheese, pasta salad, or coleslaw. Sandwiches come with potato chips, pickle, and a cookie.

THE DRIFTWOOD INN
203 Nanticoke Road
Essex, Maryland
301 / 391-3493

Business Season: all year

Hours: open daily—11 AM to 11 PM

Waterview: Hopkin's Creek / Middle River

Credit Cards: Visa, MasterCard, American Express, Choice

House Specialties: seafood platter, stuffed flounder, stuffed shrimp, crab cake platter, baked flounder, fried shrimp, clam chowder, crab soup, imperial crab, stuffed oysters

This All-American style restaurant offers strip and salisbury steak, chicken served a couple of ways, and seafood. Sitting at the long bar, I learned why this place has such a following—good food and friendly service. The crab cake platter is a delight. I also learned about a new dish to try—oysters stuffed with imperial crab, and a helpful tip—oysters are in season during the months with an "R" in them.

I enjoyed my view of the boat docks. This spot is popular with boat owners, and if you don't have a boat of your own, it's nice to watch the people who do.

RIVER WATCH RESTAURANT

207 Nanticoke Road
Essex, Maryland
301 / 687-1422

Business Season: all year

Hours: open daily—11 AM to 11 PM

Waterview: Hopkins Creek / Middle River

Credit Cards: Visa and MasterCard

House Specialties: seafood platter, surf 'n' turf, broiled scallops, crab cakes, soft shell crab, stuffed flounder, catch of the day, stuffed shrimp, oysters Rockefeller, clams casino, crab soup, oysters on the half shell, crab meat cocktail, seafood salad

Once a night club, this building with the cobblestone front and arch-shaped door is now a restaurant. Inside, several large rooms allow for plenty of light and plenty of space. A large circular bar sets the festive mood. Waitresses wear baggy khaki shorts with matching tops and deck shoes.

The dinner menu begins with crab cakes and ends with surf and turf. The two large crab cakes containing freshly picked crab meat can be prepared to your liking, either broiled or fried. The surf and turf is a 7-ounce lobster tail and a 6-ounce filet. There are 12 more seafood entrees on the menu.

Appetizers include oysters on the half shell, oysters Rockefeller, escargot, shrimp cocktail, clams casino, and crab meat cocktail. Several seafood salads are listed. One was a combination of shrimp, water chestnuts, snow peas, orange sections, and romaine lettuce all tossed and served with vinaigrette dressing. Yum!

WHITEY AND DOT'S
110 Beech Drive
Baltimore, Maryland
301 / 686-9720

Business Season: all year

Hours: Monday through Saturday—10 AM to 11 PM, Sunday—10 AM to 9 PM

Waterview: Darkhead Creek / Middle River

Credit Cards: none

House Specialties: crab cakes, fried shrimp, broiled scallops, steamed crabs, fried seafood platter

An oversized air conditioning unit that almost blocks the rear entrance of Whitey and Dot's may seem like an uninviting welcome. But step past it and go inside because the menu offers the finest in seafood at reasonable prices. You can also order from an extensive sandwich list featuring such standards as pork cutlet, breaded veal cutlet, chicken, cube steak, and beef and onion. Or try the spaghetti and meatballs. But stick with the crabs if you want the best, and enjoy the waterfront view.

WILHELM'S

1012 Beech Drive
Baltimore, Maryland
301 / 687-5080

Business Season: all year

Hours: open daily—10 AM to 11 PM

Waterview: Darkhead Creek / Middle River

Credit Cards: none

House Specialties: fried shrimp, fried seafood combination platter, soft shell crab platter, crab cakes, oysters on the half shell, fried clams

Fifty years ago this building was a grocery store that catered to visiting boaters. Today a sign on the door of the restaurant's tiny kitchen reads, "If you haven't time, please do not place order." So, plan to sit a spell. Meals are cooked to your order, and they are worth the wait.

Try Wilhelm's special steak, T-bone steak, or deluxe steak dinner. If you prefer seafood, there are eight dinners to choose from: scallops, crab cake, soft crab, oysters, fried shrimp, stuffed shrimp, a fish platter, and a seafood platter. All dinners include your choice of two vegetables and come with bread or rolls with butter. Drawbacks are that Wilhelm's has only 17 tables, and its small windows offer a limited view of the water.

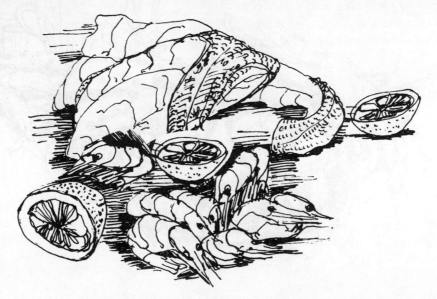

GABLER'S SHORE RESTAURANT

2200 Perryman Road
Aberdeen, Maryland
301 / 272-0626

Business Season: mid-April to 2 weeks after Labor Day

Hours: Tuesday through Friday—11 AM to 9 PM, Saturday—11 AM to 10 PM, Sunday—11 AM to 8 PM, closed Monday

Waterview: Bush River

Credit Cards: none

House Specialties: crab cakes, steamed shrimp, steamed crabs, fried shrimp, seafood platter, soft crab platter, crab salad, crab soup

Walter "Bud" Gabler recalls his first location, which was on the other side of the river: "The Bay always looks bluer on the other side." But, Bud kept his eye on the present location. That was in 1938. "All that was here were a few fishing shantys. It was all marsh land. We drained and filled and built."

Today, 121 customers can be seated inside this undistinguished looking clapboard building that faces the water over a large wooded lawn. Screened windows look out upon the narrow Bush River and the distant shore. If you don't want to eat inside, there are plenty of picnic tables outdoors and plenty of tall trees.

Bud is a magician of crustacean and spice and conjures up pots of the most wonderful steamed crabs known to humankind.

BAY STEAMER

300 Franklin Street
Havre de Grace, Maryland
301 / 939-3626

Business Season: all year

Hours: open daily—11:30 AM to 2 PM

Waterview: Susquehanna River

Credit Cards: Mastercard, Visa, American Express

House Specialties: steamed mussels, shrimp in garlic, barbecued shrimp, crab nachos, clams casino, oysters on the half shell, stuffed mushrooms, steamed shrimp, seafood salad, fettuccini neptune, crab imperial, broiled flounder, stuffed shrimp, scallops and shrimp au sherry, sauteed scallops, shrimp scampi

Named after the many Chesapeake Bay steamers that in earlier times brought traders down the beautiful Susquehanna River, the restaurant is situated on the water's edge at the foot of Franklin Street. Inside the Bay Steamer, it's so clean that it sparkles. Mirrored walls give one the illusion of space, and space is what you will need for the generous servings offered by the kitchen.

Unless you have a large appetite, you'd do best to skip over the appetizers, soup, and salad and go straight to the entrees. The chef's favorite is shrimp, lobster, and breast of chicken served over rice with snow peas, in a sauce of butter and cognac. Or you might choose chicken amaretto—chicken breast sauteed with almonds and apples and then simmered in amaretto sauce. Or try fettuccini neptune—a delicate combination of sauteed shrimp, scallops and crab, tossed with fettuccini noodles and white sauce, and topped with grated parmesan cheese.

What's steaming on the Bay? The Bay Steamer.

NORTHEAST HARBOR HOUSE

200 Cherry Street
Northeast, Maryland
301 / 287-6800

Business Season: all year

Hours: Monday through Friday—11:30 AM to 9 PM, Saturday and Sunday—8 AM to 9 PM

Waterview: Northeast River

Credit Cards: MasterCard, Visa, Choice, Diners Club, Carte Blanche

House Specialties: chicken with crab au gratin, fried seafood platter, crab imperial, crab cakes, fried shrimp, broiled scallops, broiled seafood platter, seafood bisque

The Northeast River, like so many others on the Chesapeake Bay, was first explored by Captain John Smith who found that the narrow channel led only to the head of the Bay and what is now the tiny town of Northeast. Nearby is Elkneck State Park where the landscape is so varied it goes from sandy beaches and marshland to heavily wooded bluffs that rise more than 100 feet above the river. At one time, this entire area was inhabited by tribes of Iroquois and Susquehannock Indians, and many artifacts have been found along the banks of the Northeast River.

A visit to this lovely area must include a stop at the Northeast Harbor House that offers "fine dining with a casual atmosphere." This isn't only a place for comparably priced elegant dining, but also features live entertainment. So, if you're in the mood for a soothing atmosphere and a relaxing gourmet meal, I would recommend Northeast highly.

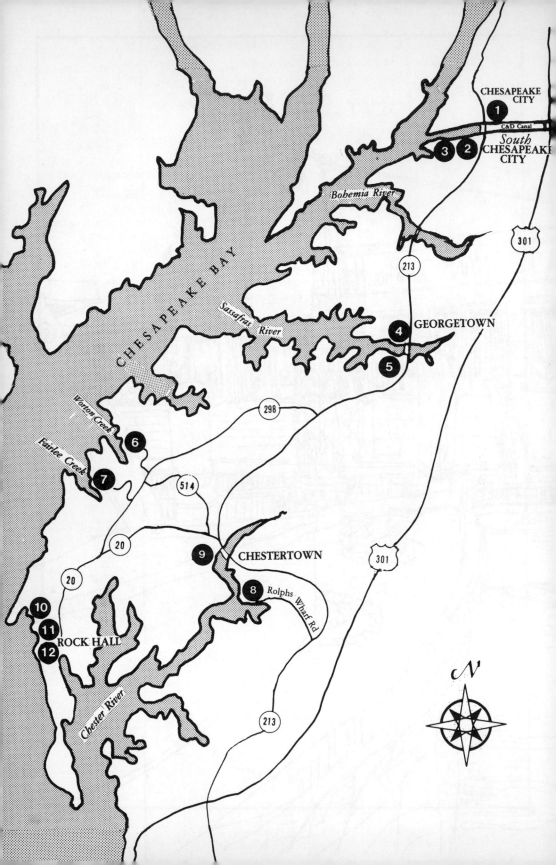

Upper Bay
Waterfront Dining

INCLUDES: Chesapeake City, South Chesapeake City, Georgetown, Chestertown, and Rock Hall, Maryland.

1. Schaefer's Canal House
2. Bayard House
3. Dockside Yacht Club Restaurant
4. The Granary
5. Kitty Knight House
6. Harbor House Restaurant
7. Mear's Great Oaks Landing
8. Rolph's Wharf Restaurant
9. Old Wharf Inn
10. Fin, Fur and Feather
11. Hubbard's Pier
12. Waterman's Crab House

SCHAEFER'S CANAL HOUSE
Bank Street
Chesapeake City, Maryland
301 / 885-2200

Business Season: all year

Hours: Monday through Saturday—11 AM to 10 PM, Sunday—11 AM to 9 PM

Waterview: Chesapeake and Delaware Canal

Credit Cards: MasterCard, Visa, American Express

House Specialties: cioppino, deviled crabs, fish of the day, oysters Rockefeller, clams casino, crab bisque, clam chowder, crab cakes, crab imperial

A popular Chesapeake Bay landmark since 1917. The following story is taken from the menu.

"...The Chesapeake and Delaware Canal, which links the upper reaches of the Chesapeake Bay with the Delaware River, was first proposed in 1661 by Augustine Herman, the Dutch envoy from New Amsterdam (New York) to St. Marys in Maryland. Herman, a mapmaker and surveyor, was at the time about half-way through a ten-year-long project to map the Delmarva Peninsula.

"At the time, however, there was no United States. The task of becoming united absorbed the several states during the next two decades, and it was not until 1788 that the matters were well enough under control to allow the idea of a canal to again be raised.

"Finally, on 17 October 1829 the Chesapeake and Delaware Canal Company, No. 44 Walnut Street, Philadelphia, Pennsylvania, was able to announce that its canal was open and ready for business. The canal at the time was 13 miles long, had a waterline width of 66 feet, a bottom width of 36 feet, and a depth of 10 feet.

"In 1921 the Army Engineers began work on a $10,710,000 project to widen the canal 90 feet, deepen it to 12 feet, provide a new and straighter eastern entrance to Reedy Point, Delaware (about two miles south of the original entrance), excavate some 16,000,000 cubic yards of material, remove the locks, and construct one railroad and four highway lift bridges. The face lifting operation was completed in 1927."

So why not go to Schaefer's and enjoy a slice of history on the Chesapeake and Delaware Canal?

BAYARD HOUSE

11 Bohemia Street
South Chesapeake City, Maryland
301 / 885-5040

Business Season: all year

Hours: Monday through Saturday—lunch 11:30 AM to 2:30 PM,
Monday through Thursday—dinner 5 PM to 9 PM, Friday and
Saturday—dinner 5 PM to 10 PM, Sunday—1 PM to 8 PM

Waterview: Chesapeake and Delaware Canal

Credit Cards: MasterCard, Visa, American Express

House Specialties: crab cakes, crab imperial, surf'n'turf, broiled
shrimp, broiled scallops

If you are interested in history, you will enjoy reading the story the
menu tells:

"Welcome to the Bayard House! This beautifully restored Inn has
witnessed many years of warm hospitality. The original brick part of the
Inn was built around 1815 to 1820 and was referred to as the Back Creek
House in an 1829 survey. A frame addition was added in 1845 and Sarah
Beaston, owner and builder, sold it to Richard H. Bayard and his wife,
May Sophia. Captain Firman Layman, who lived next door to the Inn,
operated the hotel under the name of 'Bayard House' until 1881. When
the Harriott family took it over, they renamed it the 'Harriott Hotel.' The
'Harriott Hotel' was so popular and crowded that the beds had to be rented
in shifts. The bar was called 'The-Hole-in-the-Wall,' because one of its walls
had a hole through which drinks were served to be consumed outside.
The dining room was noted for fine food at affordable prices, a tradition
still true today.

"This handsome brick Inn considered to be the earliest building in
Chesapeake City, has been lovingly restored. No details were spared including the locks on the doors, which are replicas of the two original ones found
in the attic.

"After you are finished with your meal, take a few minutes to visit
tranquil Chesapeake City, formerly known as 'Bohemia Village.' Once it
was a lively port, a commercial crossroad, where boats loaded and unloaded
their goods from the Canal.''

DOCKSIDE YACHT CLUB RESTAURANT

On the Canal
South Chesapeake City, Maryland
301 / 885-5016

Business Season: March to mid November

Hours: Wednesday, Thursday, and Sunday—11 AM to 9 PM; Friday and Saturday—11 AM to 10 PM

Waterview: Chesapeake and Delaware Canal

Credit Cards: MasterCard, Visa, American Express

House Specialties: crab imperial, crab cakes, soft shell crab platter, shrimp scampi, broiled scallops, coconut shrimp

The newest offering on the luncheon menu is from the land— mesquite grilled to order on French bread and served with natural fries and horseradish sauce. If you prefer a selection from the sea, then let it be the golden baked crab, a delicate combination of fresh crab meat, secret seasonings, tomato slices, and cheddar cheese sauce, all baked on a Thomas' English muffin, with a side dish of salad or cole slaw. Or, you may try the coconut shrimp. Here the entree is dipped in a pina colada batter, rolled in coconut, and deep fried. The results are incredibly delicious.

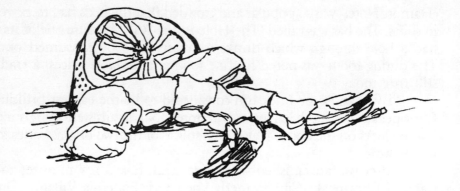

THE GRANARY
Route 213
Georgetown, Maryland
301 / 275-8177

Business Season: all year

Hours: Monday through Thursday—lunch 11 AM to 3 PM, dinner 5 PM to 9 PM; Friday and Saturday—lunch 11 AM to 3 PM, dinner 5 PM to 10 PM; Sunday—1 PM to 8 PM

Waterview: Sassafras River

Credit Cards: American Express, Visa, MasterCard

House Specialties: crab soup, crab cakes, seafood platter, clams or oysters on the half shell, oysters Rockefeller, smoked fish du jour, crab meat cocktail, crab imperial

The menu's cover gives some interesting information:
"In 1812 the residents of Frederick Town erected on this site Fort Duffy, one of several forts that served as the county's defense against the British. In 1813, however, the town and its fort were burned by a British fleet consisting of 'fifteen barges and three small boats.' The twin village of Georgetown (both communities being named after the two sons of King George II) was also burned.

"Several years later the granary was built. Existing records date back only as far as 1876, when the building was purchased by Ben Walmsley. Walmsley stored corn and grain for shipment to Baltimore.

"This building was opened as a restaurant in the late 1940's, utilizing the original grain bins and warehouse as part of the dining facilities. Prior to this time, it housed the old Tockwogh Yacht Club ' Tockwogh' is an Indian word meaning 'Sassafras.'

"Sadly, this original structure was destroyed by fire in March 1985. The hand-hewn beams in the vestibule are all that remains of the 'old' Granary. The 'new' Granary, overlooking the Sassafras River, continues to offer relaxed fine dining in a gracious manner."

KITTY KNIGHT HOUSE

Route 213
Georgetown, Maryland
301 / 648-5777

Business Season: all year

Hours: lunch—11:30 AM to 2 PM, dinner—5:30 PM to 10 PM

Waterview: Sassafras River

Credit Cards: Visa, MasterCard, American Express

House Specialties: crab cake platter, crab imperial, oysters on the half shell, crab meat cocktail, shrimp scampi, crab bisque, clams on the half shell, broiled flounder filet, fried oysters

The menu tells the story:

"Often described as 'one of the most beautiful women ever born and raised in Kent County,' Kitty Knight's regal stature and infinite grace dazzled many in her day, including George Washington with whom she claims to have once danced.

"But it is her great heroism during the War of 1812, not her renown as a society belle, that has earned her an everlasting place in Maryland history.

"In May of 1813, British troops advanced up the Sassafras River, leaving in their wake entire towns reduced to ash. Georgetown residents, hearing the news, quickly fled their approach, rescuing whatever valuable belongings they could carry.

"Miss Kitty Knight, however, stayed to protect her invalid neighbor who was too ill to move. Defying Admiral Sir George Cockburn, she firmly planted her feet and declared, 'I shall not leave. If you burn this house, you burn me with it.'

"After several attempts to persuade her to leave, the British finally relented.

"Once the smoke had cleared, these two brick houses at the top of the hill (presently joined to form what is now the Kitty Knight House) were the only residences left standing.

"The Kitty Knight House Restaurant offers a complete menu selection featuring an exciting mix of both traditional local favorites and select continental cuisine.

"Using only the freshest, choicest ingredients, your meal is carefully prepared under the watchful eye of Executive Chef David L. Banks. All of our meats and fish are hand selected and cut daily; vegetables are always fresh."

HARBOR HOUSE RESTAURANT
Buck Neck Road
Chestertown, Maryland
301 / 778-0669

Business Season: May 1 through October 31

Hours: Wednesday through Sunday—dinner from 5:30 PM, closed Tuesday

Waterview: Worton Creek / Chesapeake Bay

Credit Cards: Visa and MasterCard

House Specialties: crab cakes, soft shell crabs, crab imperial, fresh fish of the day, broiled shrimp, scallops, clams in herb butter

"Sweet as a woman's kiss and tender as her lips" best describes the seafood dishes served at the the Harbor House Restaurant. Located in a lovely wooded setting, Harbor House overlooks the narrow Worton Creek and offers a view from above the marina. The day I went there, the gentle curve of land and water was bright with the setting sun, but my seat at one of the large windows was shaded by the groves of lovely trees.

There was no printed menu, the day's specials were listed on an artist's easel and placed at the end of the table for all to see. I was greeted by the manager, Martha Hughes, who told me of the soups of the day. And what a delight they were—Greek lemon soup, peppered cauliflower soup, and wild mushroom soup. My appetizer, pasta with a red clam sauce, was exceptionally fresh, colorful, and tasty. My entree was one of the best crab cakes I have ever had the occasion to try, surrounded by a succulent soft shell crab cooked to perfection. It was accompanied by a medley of home grown vegetables plus a loaf of bread hot and fresh from the oven.

It's all here—a quiet harbor, a lovely view, friendly people, and fine dining. The candlelight and soft background music combine to create a comfortably sophisticated atmosphere in which to enjoy your eastern shore dinner. I can't wait to return.

MEAR'S GREAT OAK LANDING

Handy Point Road
Chestertown, Maryland
301 / 778-2100

Business Season: year round

Hours: open daily—7 AM to 10 PM

Waterview: Fairlee Creek / Chesapeake Bay

Credit Cards: MasterCard, Visa, Choice, American Express

House Specialties: filet of flounder, imperial stuffed shrimp, jumbo lump crab cakes, broiled sea scallops, mariners platter, oysters on the half shell, clams on the half shell, oyster stew

Mear's Great Oak Landing Restaurant is part of a hilltop lodge that overlooks the well-protected Fairlee Creek. Conveniently located for family outings or business meetings, the lodge provides a golf course, yacht club, complete marina, pond sanctuary and superb accommodations.

Enjoy your fine dining while you view the Creek through the large windows of the long, narrow dining room. Canadian geese are a frequent sight.

ROLPH'S WHARF RESTAURANT
Rolph's Wharf Road
Chestertown, Maryland
301 / 778-3227

Business Season: all year

Hours: Wednesday through Sunday—lunch 11 AM to 3 PM, dinner 5 PM to 10 PM, closed Monday and Tuesday

Waterview: Chester River

Credit Cards: Visa and MasterCard

House Specialties: broiled flounder, crab cakes, crab imperial, scallops, stuffed shrimp, steamed shrimp, broiled lobster tail

The Chesapeake Bay traveler wins when he pays a visit to Rolph's Wharf, a combined marina, restaurant, and country inn. At the water's edge is a large birdhouse where purple martins and sparrows compete for space. The grounds have a picnic area that is a deck surrounding a large tree in the center of the lawn, and there are lots of lovely old cedar trees. The view from Rolph's Point looks out to Devil's Reach and over onto Skillet Point, once a steamboat stop between Chestertown and Baltimore.

On Thursday, try the ''all you can eat'' steamed shrimp. On Friday, the special is lobster tail, and on Saturday, ''all you can eat'' seafood buffet.

OLD WHARF INN

Cannon Street
Chestertown, Maryland
301 / 778-3055

Business Season: all year

Hours: Monday through Thursday—11 AM to 9 PM, Friday and Saturday—11 AM to 10 PM, Sunday—12 noon to 9 PM

Waterview: Chester River

Credit Cards: Visa and MasterCard

House Specialties: fried shrimp, crab cakes, crab imperial, baked stuffed shrimp, fried seafood platter, steamed platter, fresh flounder stuffed with crab imperial

Located at the foot of Cannon Street, the Old Wharf Inn is just a block and a half from the center of town. For John Linville, who once worked for the previous owner, it is a dream come true. When the restaurant went up for sale, he was willing to step right in as owner, and under his guiding light, the menu shines in all departments.

There are 17 seafood entrees available. One that looked good to me at a recent visit was a seafood platter consisting of crab cake, shrimp, fried clams, broiled fish, and imperial crab. It was piled high and inviting. If you prefer fresh fish, look at the blackboard for the catch of the day. The fish will be served with your choice of sauce. Since I have lived in Virginia for a good part of my life, I have grown fond of Smithfield ham and, when I saw it listed on the menu, I couldn't resist ordering it. Entrees are served with salad and your choice of baked potato, wedge-cut french fries, rice pilaf, cole slaw, stewed tomatoes with eggplant, or the vegetable du jour. Those with small appetites will appreciate a special feature that Mr. Linville offers, petite portions. Top off your meal with dessert, which can provide a small celebration in itself.

FIN, FUR, AND FEATHER

424 Bayside Avenue
Rock Hall, Maryland
301 / 639-7454

Business Season: all year

Hours: Monday through Thursday—9 AM to 9 PM, Friday and
Saturday—8 AM to 10 PM, Sunday—8 AM to 8 PM, closed
daily—3 PM to 5 PM

Waterview: Rock Hall Harbor

Credit Cards: none

House Specialties: fisherman's chowder, crab soup, clam chowder,
oyster stew, steamed oysters, stuffed shrimp, fried clam strips,
soft shell crabs, broiled oysters, fish of the day

The menu tells the story: "Our seafood is fresh and made to order.
Please allow our cooks time to prepare your food. It cannot be rushed.
When available, our seafood is bought from Rock Hall watermen." If you
count the soups and appetizers, there are 37 ways that the seafood can
be enjoyed. Try this restaurant, and you won't be disappointed.

Rock Hall is beautiful any time of the year, but many people say that
their favorite time to go is in the fall when geese, ducks, and swans darken
the sunset sky; they are your companions during the day's journey. Great
V-shaped flocks of Canada geese migrate by the tens of thousands, many
to settle on Maryland's eastern shore to spend the winter. In the spring,
the geese will return to their nesting grounds up north.

HUBBARD'S PIER

Hawthorne Avenue
Rock Hall, Maryland
301 / 778-4700

Business Season: all year

Hours: open daily—4 AM to 8 PM

Waterview: Rock Hall Harbor

Credit Cards: none

House Specialties: crab cakes, soft shell crabs, fried scallops, fried clams, broiled fish of the day, crab soup, oyster stew, clam chowder, seafood combination platter

A good seafood restaurant learns to adapt to changing times, and that's what Hubbard's has done. You see, "rockfish" was once the signature item on the menu, but with the rockfish ban, they simply crossed it out and continued on with good down-home cooking. The service is fast and pleasant. As for the location and the view—well, when I'm at Hubbard's, I wouldn't want to be anywhere else. Visit, and I'm sure that you'll agree.

WATERMAN'S CRAB HOUSE
Sharp Street Wharf
Rock Hall, Maryland
301 / 639-2261

Business Season: all year

Hours: open daily—4 AM to 10 PM

Waterview: Rock Hall Harbor

Credit Cards: none

House Specialties: steamed crabs, crab cakes, crab imperial, fish dinner, fried seafood combination platter, soft shell crab sandwich

What's nice about Rock Hall is that it is a working harbor and, in the winter, there is warmth in eating the oyster stews and chowders; in the summer, there is ice on the frosted mug; and there are always pleasant people to meet and interesting things to see.

The town of Rock Hall dates to the early 1700's and once linked a ferry line that stretched from New York to the Carolinas. Today it remains a unique stop to all Chesapeake Bay travelers. At Waterman's Crab House, owned by Wayne Brady, you can sit looking out at the harbor and dream of those bygone eras.

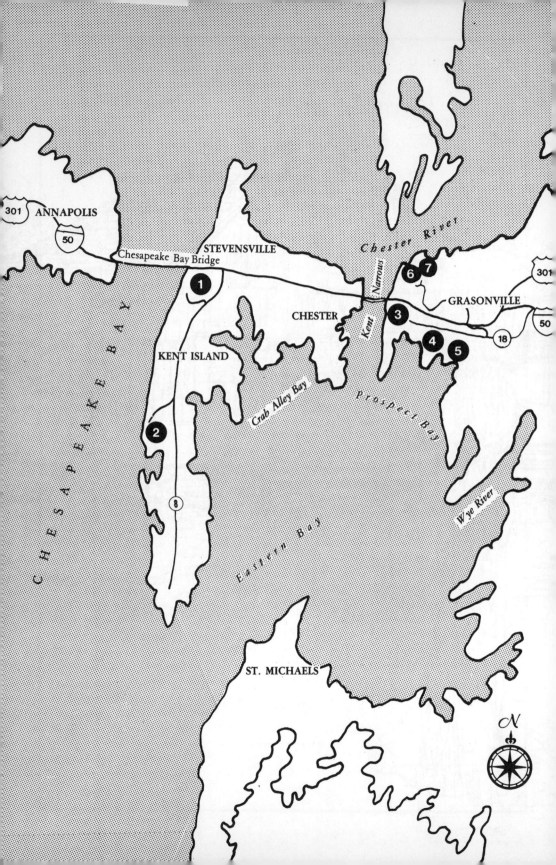

Kent Island

Waterfront Dining

INCLUDES: Stevensville, Grasonville, and Kent Island, Maryland.

1. Hemingway's Seafood Restaurant
2. Kentmorr Harbour Restaurant
3. Anglers Inn
4. The Narrows
5. Fisherman's Inn Restaurant
6. Harris Crab House
7. Poseidon Restaurant

HEMINGWAY'S SEAFOOD RESTAURANT

Pier One Marina Road
Stevensville, Maryland
301 / 643-2722
or 643-2196

Business Season: all year

Hours: Monday through Saturday—11 AM to 10 PM, Sunday—9 AM to 10 PM

Waterview: Chesapeake Bay

Credit Cards: Visa, MasterCard, American Express, Choice, Diners Club, Discover

House Specialties: clams casino, steamed mussels or shrimp, clam chowder, seafood salad, stuffed shrimp, crab cakes, crab imperial, seafood Norfolk, broiled flounder

This is surely one of the most impressive restaurant settings in the state. You approach it along a winding driveway and, at the foot of the William Preston Lane, Jr. Memorial Bridge (also known as the Bay Bridge), amid spacious grounds, stands Hemingway's, its windows aglow with candlelight.

Inside, the food is imaginatively prepared and beautifully served. The menu contains a dozen appetizers, the specialty being barbecued shrimp cooked to your order. Notable entrees include baked shrimp or chicken, both stuffed with crab. The seafood sampler dinner brings the most raves. Owner David Harper starts you off with a fresh garden salad with your choice of dressing, lots of hot rolls with butter, baked stuffed potato or ranch fries, fried clams, fried oysters, crab cakes, fresh broiled flounder, steamed shrimp, soft shell crabs, mussels, and steamed clams, garnished with lemon, tartar sauce, and cocktail sauce.

While you are enjoying this incredible feast, take note that the bridge crosses the Bay in a long arc, this being necessary to comply with federal regulations stating that a bridge must cross at right angles to the main ship channel. Here are a few other interesting facts. The eastern channel span for both structures is 780 feet with a roadway height of 63 feet above mean high water. The length of the original span is 4.02 miles; the parallel span is 3.98 miles. The annual traffic volume on the bridge is about 10 million vehicles.

KENTMORR HARBOUR RESTAURANT

Kentmorr Road
Stevensville, Maryland
301 / 643-4700
or 643-3337

Business Season: last week in February through November

Hours: Tuesday through Sunday—11 AM to 11 PM, closed Monday

Waterview: Chesapeake Bay

Credit Cards: Visa and MasterCard

House Specialties: crab cakes, crab imperial, soft crab platter, steamed crab, barbequed shrimp, crab soup, cream of crab soup, soft shell clams, cherry stone clams, crab balls

Visitors to Stevensville, located on the Isle of Kent, soon learn that few marinas can offer the varied atmosphere that the Kentmorr Marina has to offer. The island has an interesting history. It was settled in 1631 by William Claiborne from Virginia, and under his direction, soon gained considerable economic importance. Tobacco was its first crop, and later furs became a prime source of income. Today, fishing, farming, and fine foods are the island's major resources.

After one of those bad winter seasons (when the Chesapeake Bay was practically frozen over), Kentmorr Harbor Restaurant owner David Wehrs took a sledge hammer and knocked out a wall to expose a broadside view of the Bay. This led to major renovations. He put in new windows and a fireplace, enclosed the old side porch, extended the bar, connected the lighting, and painted and filled the pool.

Today, you can feast on the restaurant's excellent steamed crabs and Maryland lump crab cakes. Then play volley ball on the lawn or take wind-surfing lessons on the Bay.

ANGLERS INN
Route 18
Grasonville, Maryland
301 / 827-6717

Business Season: all year

Hours: open daily—5 AM to 10 PM

Waterview: Kent Narrows / Prospect Bay

Credit Cards: none

House Specialties: soft crab sandwich, steamed crabs, seafood platter, crab cake, fried shrimp, oyster stew, crab soup, clam chowder

Bert and Cass Droter are your hosts at this delightful, down-home, hole-in-the-wall place about the size of a matchbox—straight out of the American scene of 40 years ago, only better. It is sought out constantly by locals and Bay travelers who hunger for earthy watermen's dishes. In addition to the likes of fresh soft shell crab sandwiches, try any of the specials of the day. A recent listing included shrimp, crab, oysters, scallops, and clams. YUM!

THE NARROWS
Route 50 at Kent Narrows
Grasonville, Maryland
301 / 827-8113

Business Season: all year

Hours: 11 AM to 10 PM, weekends—11 AM to 11 PM, Sunday brunch—11 AM to 2 PM

Waterview: Kent Narrows / Prospect Bay

Credit Cards: Visa, MasterCard, Diners Club, Carte Blanche

House Specialties: crab soup, crab cakes, crab imperial, soft shell crab, soft shell clams, breaded oysters, shrimp scampi, fish of the day

The Narrows menu tells the story:
"Stunning sunsets and fresh breezes grace The Narrows Restaurant on its Kent Narrows waterfront vista. Opened in the fall of 1983, the 'Narrows' is a graceful and appropriate replacement for the former shucking house.

"Resting on 'erster' shells, pilings, and concrete, The Narrows brings the eastern shore's unique sights and sounds to each of its guests. Traditional oyster, crab, and clam workboats ply the waters of Kent Narrows daily among flocks of ducks, swans, and migrating geese. Watermen unload and cull their catches on nearby docks in the time-honored patterns of the shore. In sharp contrast, sleek and fashionable sail and power boats cut through Kent Narrows on their way to ports throughout the Bay.

"The Narrows features traditional Maryland recipes that take advantage of Eastern Shore harvests."

FISHERMAN'S INN RESTAURANT
Route 50 and 301
Grasonville, Maryland
301 / 827-8807

Business Season: all year

Hours: open daily—11 AM to 10 PM

Waterview: Kent Narrows / Prospect Bay

Credit Cards: American Express, Visa, Choice, Master Card

House Specialties: crab meat cocktail, clams on the half shell, baked clams casino, crab soup, cream of crab soup, clam chowder, seafood salad platter, broiled seafood platter, baked imperial crab, fried seafood platter, combination of soft crab and crab cakes

Swirling waters separate Kent Island from the mainland of the eastern shore and mark the northern juncture of the Eastern Bay and the Chesapeake Bay. The area is a center for fishing, oystering, clamming, and crabbing, and a front row seat to view this activity is at the Fisherman's Inn, "a tradition since 1930."

Mention the word "oyster" to food connoisseurs in the Bay area, and their eyes will sparkle. Mention the words "oyster plate" to Sonny and Betty Schulz, owners of the Fisherman's Inn, and they will be happy to show off the room that they have decorated with a collection of these plates. During the Victorian period, if you bought the very best china, oyster plates were included with a service of dinnerware. Now they are hard to find. In considering oyster plates as a potential for a beginning collector, Mrs. Schulz warns that you should expect the prices to be somewhat high because the demand for these beautiful items is much higher than the supply.

HARRIS CRAB HOUSE

Sewards Point Road
Grasonville, Maryland
301 / 827-8104

Business Season: all year

Hours: Sunday through Thursday—11 AM to 9 PM, Friday and Saturday—11 AM to 10 PM

Waterview: Kent Narrows / Chester River

Credit Cards: none

House Specialties: steamed crabs, seafood platter, crab cakes, flounder, fried shrimp, soft crab sandwich, cream of crab soup

Opening in 1948, this restaurant has since then established itself as a local favorite for good food, good drink, and good service. Captain Bill Harris is sure to give both the public and the boating crowd a true flavor of the old eastern shore.

Along with excellent steamed crabs, the Captain also offers steamed shrimp, soft shell clams, and cherrystone clams. The "Harris Seafood Basket" is one of my favorites. It includes 11 shrimp, 6 cherrystone clams, 12 soft shell clams, king crab legs, and 2 ears of corn. Look forward to Tuesday and Thursday nights with their "all you can eat" special served from 6 to 9 PM.

You are welcome to come dressed casually and eat inside or outside on the deck. Enjoy the friendly atmosphere. Captain Harris asks that you be patient— it takes time to prepare good food. We agree.

POSEIDON RESTAURANT

Route 50 and 301 at Kent Narrows
Grasonville, Maryland
301 / 827-7605

Business Season: all year

Hours: open daily—11 AM to 11 PM, Sunday brunch—11 AM to 2 PM

Waterview: Kent Narrows

Credit Cards: American Express, Visa, MasterCard

House Specialties: oysters on the half shell, shrimp cocktail, crab meat cocktail, clams casino, cream of crab soup, filet of flounder, imperial stuffed shrimp, seafood sampler, crab cakes, crab imperial, barbecued shrimp

This restaurant, featuring regional delicacies in a picturesque nautical setting, is located 5 miles east of the Bay Bridge at the Mear's Point Marina. Whether you come by land or by sea, the Poseidon has something to offer everyone. A completely renovated yachting resort, it is now bigger and better than ever. You will be pleasantly surprised by its warmth and charm. It is beautifully decorated and well worth the visit.

I spent a lovely summer evening gazing out over the water's edge munching on the delicious appetizers. Since my group couldn't decide to order, we ended up sharing the oysters Poseidon (large succulent oysters topped with crab imperial and baked to perfection) and the barbecued shrimp (wrapped in bacon and grilled in a zesty sauce), each served over rice.

If you have a small appetite, beware! The sensational salads are meals in themselves. You can choose from a list of five. I liked the seafood Caesar best. It included romaine, crab, shrimp, lobster, hard-boiled egg, tomato, onion, anchovy, olives, and croutons.

Entrees include fresh filet of flounder, imperial stuffed shrimp, jumbo lump crab cakes, and backfin crab imperial. Not one of us had room for dessert, but the management offered to pack it for travel. They knew we'd want some later. The day's listings included chocolate cake, custard napoleons, exotic fruit tarts, chocolate eclairs, and super scoop ice cream sundaes.

St. Michaels
Waterfront Dining

INCLUDES: *St. Michaels, Tilghman Island, and Oxford, Maryland.*

1. Lighthouse Restaurant
2. Longfellow's Restaurant
3. Town Dock Restaurant
4. The Crab Claw Restaurant
5. The Inn at Perry Cabin
6. Harbour Watch Restaurant
7. Bay Hundred Restaurant
8. The Bridge Restaurant
9. The Tilghman Inn
10. Harrison's Chesapeake House
11. Town Creek Restaurant
12. Pier Street Restaurant

LIGHTHOUSE RESTAURANT
101 North Harbour Road
St. Michaels, Maryland
301 / 745-9001

Business Season: all year

Hours: open daily—breakfast 7 AM to 11 AM, lunch 11 AM to 2 PM, dinner 5 PM to 9 PM, Sunday—brunch 10 AM to 2 PM

Waterview: St. Michaels Harbor/Miles River

Credit Cards: Visa and MasterCard

House Specialties: crab cakes, stuffed shrimp, catch of the day, shrimp scampi, soft shell crab, crab imperial, baked flounder, sauteed crab meat, baked stuffed flounder

"The newest pride of the eastern shore," the Lighthouse Restaurant, is part of St. Michaels Harbour Inn and Marina. It got its name from being located across from the Chesapeake Bay Maritime Museum's famed "Hooper Straight" Lighthouse. Set on the second floor, this beautiful glass-enclosed restaurant overlooks the harbor. But the Lighthouse offers more than just a good look at water, boats, a swimming pool, and buildings.

Take a look at the engaging menu. Begin with the appetizers: fresh oysters on the half shell, clams casino, or Maryland lump crab meat cocktail. Then try the soups: she crab, oyster stew, or onion soup au gratin. Follow this with a tossed mixed green salad.

Entrees include a bountiful assortment of traditional Maryland favorites. When my baked stuffed flounder arrived, the waitress quickly cautioned, "Be careful, the plate is hot." Savory crab meat with fine spices and a tasty lemon butter sauce topped the delicate boneless filet. This fresh catch of the day was cooked to perfection.

Enjoy the fine food, relaxing atmosphere, and charming bar. This is Maryland's eastern shore cooking at its best. I can't wait to return.

LONGFELLOW'S RESTAURANT
125 Mulberry Street
St. Michaels, Maryland
301 / 745-2624

Business Season: all year

Hours: Sunday through Thursday—10 AM to 10 PM, Friday and Saturday—10 AM to 11 PM

Waterview: St. Michaels Harbor / Miles River

Credit Cards: MasterCard, Visa, Choice

House Specialties: broiled seafood platter, baked stuffed shrimp, sauteed soft shell crabs, crab imperial, oyster stew, oysters on the half shell

You can read about Longfellow's seafood dishes and desserts in the magazines *Bon Appetite, Southern Living,* and *Essence.* Once you arrive in St. Michaels, however, you'll find that this restaurant is not the only attraction. The menu tells about some of the others.

"St. Michaels is a little town on the eastern shore with a big history. Her picturesque tree-lined streets, comfortable homes, and narrow brick walkways provide visitors with a relaxed unhurried setting.

"Hailed as the birthplace of the illustrious Baltimore clipper and racing log canoe, St. Michaels, famous since colonial times as a ship-building capital, is still going strong today. Her harbor continues to provide her citizens with their source of livelihood. A recent addition to the harbor scene is the famed Chesapeake Bay Maritime Museum. Exhibits include an authentic Chesapeake Bay lighthouse, comprehensive bay-craft collection, boat restoration shop, extensive waterfowl decoy collection, aquarium featuring life from local waters, and several restored period houses.

"Throughout the year, the historic Miles River plays host to pleasure boats and commercial fishing, clamming, and oystering vessels. In the autumn, its shores are visited by thousands of geese, swans, and ducks, all adding to the excitement of shore life."

A town truly steeped in maritime tradition, St. Michaels is a delightful example of what the eastern shore is all about.

TOWN DOCK RESTAURANT

305 Mulberry Street
St. Michaels, Maryland
301 / 745-5577

Business Season: all year

Hours: open daily—lunch 11:30 AM to 4 PM, dinner 4 PM to 10 PM, Sunday brunch 9:30 AM to 1 PM

Waterview: St. Michaels Harbor / Miles River

Credit Cards: Visa and MasterCard

House Specialties: crab cakes, crab imperial, flounder stuffed with crab imperial, shrimp scampi, cioppino, sword fish au gratin, cream of crab bisque, seafood chowder, steamed crabs

Here is some interesting information from the menu.

"Welcome to the Town Dock Marina and Restaurant and St. Michaels Harbor. The Town Dock Restaurant and Marina have been the unloading site for millions of oysters and crabs distributed from Boston to the Carolinas. The watermen in this area have worked laboriously for hundreds of years...often in inclement weather and untenable conditions...to ensure a plentiful supply of eastern shore seafood specialties.

"The building which houses the Town Dock Lounge dates back to the 1830's when it served as one of St. Michaels earliest oyster shucking sheds. Inspect the lounge ceiling joists for authenticity. The patio bricks outside the Town Dock Restaurant were kilned in St. Michaels during the late 1800's. It has been reported the anchors in the landscape area of the Town Dock patio moored the ships of old that sailed the Chesapeake waters. Feel free to visit our lounge and patio and meet the numerous watermen, artists, entertainers, townfolk, politicians, and yachtsmen that visit this area."

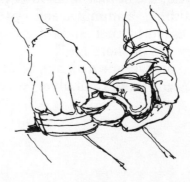

THE CRAB CLAW RESTAURANT
Navy Point
St. Michaels, Maryland
301 / 745-2900

Business Season: March 17 through November 13

Hours: Tuesday through Sunday—11 AM to 10 PM, closed Monday except open for lunch April 14 through Labor Day

Waterview: St. Michaels Harbor / Miles River

Credit Cards: none

House Specialties: crab claws, oysters on the half shell, clams casino, oysters casino, crab soup, clam chowder, seafood platters, crab imperial, crab cakes, soft shell crabs, fried hard crab, fried clams

Are you fascinated by tales of the sea and the brave men who sailed upon it? Do you enjoy watching the seamen of today challenge Mother Nature on the Chesapeake Bay? Do steamed crabs, freshly shucked oysters, and creamy crab soup make your mouth water and your eyes sparkle?

If you answer yes to any of these questions, come visit The Crab Claw and see what you have been missing. It is located beside the Chesapeake Bay Maritime Museum on Navy Point overlooking St. Michaels Harbor. You will enjoy your visit to the town, for St. Michaels has something for everyone. Whether you come for a day, a weekend, or longer, you'll be glad you came, sorry to leave, and sure to return.

THE INN AT PERRY CABIN
308 Watkins Lane
St. Michaels, Maryland
301 / 745-5178

Business Season: all year

Hours: Monday through Saturday—11 AM to 11 PM, Sunday—12 noon to 10 PM

Waterview: Miles River

Credit Cards: Visa, MasterCard, Choice, American Express

House Specialties: clams casino, oysters on the half shell, crab meat in mushroom caps, cream of crab soup, crab imperial, soft shell crab, seafood platter

Inside the Inn, three elegant dining rooms reveal a remarkable view of the Miles River. Soft candle light, a cozy fireplace, and the sound of wild geese on moonlit waters create a comfortable atmosphere. Luncheons are served in the Bid Bar, once a carriage house, where the decor includes thoroughbred-racing memorabilia from the collection of the Meyerhoff family.

The menu's cover tells about the restaurant's history:

"The Inn at Perry Cabin is one of the eastern shore's most distinguished historic sites. Perry Cabin was built in the early 1800's by Samuel Hambleton, a purser in the U.S. Navy. Hambleton served directly under Commodore Oliver Hazard Perry on Perry's flagship, the Lawrence, during the War of 1812. It was Commodore Perry who, upon defeating the British in the Battle of Lake Erie, sent the now famous communique, 'We have met the enemy and they are ours.' Samuel Hambleton so admired Perry that he named his residence after him.

"In 1909 Perry Cabin was transformed from a private residence to an inn and later served as a riding academy. In 1928 it was used as the location for the filming of a silent film, *The First Kiss*, starring Fay Wray and Gary Cooper.

"Today the Inn stands open to the public for dining and overnight lodging in a setting restored as closely as possible to the way it was when Samual Hambleton first lived here over 150 years ago."

HARBOUR WATCH RESTAURANT
Route 33
St. Michaels, Maryland
301 / 745-9066

Business Season: all year

Hours: open daily—breakfast 7 AM to 11 AM, lunch 11 AM to 4 PM, dinner 5 PM to 9 PM

Waterview: Miles River

Credit Cards: Visa, MasterCard, American Express

House Specialties: crab meat cocktail, cream of crab soup, crab imperial, shrimp and crab Norfolk, shrimp and pasta, broiled seafood ensemble

The Harbour Watch Restaurant is part of the Martingham Harbour-towne Inn Resort / Conference Facility located on the Miles River about one mile outside of St. Michaels. There you will find 573 acres with 4.5 miles of waterfront where wild fowl, natural beaches, and woodlands provide attractive subject matter for both photographers and artists. Open to the public for breakfast, lunch, and dinner, the restaurant's excellent Saturday night buffet and Sunday brunch bring the most raves.

BAY HUNDRED RESTAURANT
Route 33
Tilghman Island, Maryland
301 / 886-2622

Business Season: all year

Hours: open daily—lunch 11 AM to 3:30 PM, dinner 5:30 PM to 10 PM

Waterview: Knapp's Narrows

Credit Cards: MasterCard and Visa

House Specialties: seafood combination, fresh fish of the day, shrimp scampi, crab cakes, soft crabs, stir fried shrimp, crab soup, crab salad, roasted oysters, oyster stew

For an imaginative menu with a personal touch, try Bay Hundred. The fresh fish, priced daily, is a filet basted with butter, chargrilled, and served with the potato of the day. All dinner entrees come with a house salad, fresh vegetable, and a loaf of bread. At a recent visit, I decided to try the roast oysters. Through a window, we watched the cook roast the oysters outside and, I must admit, they were the finest of the season. That, plus a view of all the boats, made for a delightful evening. I can't wait to return.

Dickson J. Preston's *Talbot County, A History* provides an interesting historical background: "By the 1670's Talbot County...had been divided for administrative purposes into 'hundreds,' each with its own constable. These districts were survivors from medieval times in Britain when shires were marked off into segments that could produce a hundred fighting men apiece. 'Bay Hundred,' the old name for the Tilghman peninsula, continues in use today."

THE BRIDGE RESTAURANT
Route 33
Tilghman Island, Maryland
301 / 886-2500

Business Season: all year, closed Christmas

Hours: Monday through Thursday—12 noon to 9 PM, Friday through Sunday—12 noon to 10 PM

Waterview: Knapps Narrows

Credit Cards: American Express, Visa, MasterCard

House Specialties: oyster stew, oysters on the half shell, crab cakes, soft shell crabs, oyster fritters, crab balls, cream of crab soup, crab soup, oyster pie, seafood buffet, baked scallops, baked stuffed shrimp

If you are traveling there by car, you will enjoy the scenic drive from the Chesapeake Bay Bridge. Bypass Easton and turn right onto Route 322, and right again onto Route 33. Then continue straight through St. Michaels till you reach Tilghman Island. Offer yourself a change of pace as you watch the busiest drawbridge in the world. Take the time to walk the docks and talk to the watermen, bring your camera or sketch pad, and enjoy a truly relaxing adventure.

Then dine at The Bridge Restaurant. Reservations are suggested if you'd like the Friday night buffet or the best seller, the seafood combination.

"FRIDAY SEAFOOD BONANZA BUFFET

Soup du Jour • Lobster, Oyster and Scallops Newburg • Fish du Jour • Oyster Crepes — fresh oysters sauteed and simmered in a light wine and cheese sauce • Shrimp Creole with saffron rice • Steamship Round of Beef carved to order • Steamed Shrimp • Salad bar with choice of delicious dressings • Assorted Breads with butter..."

If all this isn't enough, I must tell you that the owner, Francis Cole, was one of those adventurous investors who helped Mel Fisher find millions in gold pieces, gems, and silver aboard "The Atocha." Some of that treasure is on view at The Bridge. It's worth seeing!

THE TILGHMAN INN
Coopertown Road
Tilghman Island, Maryland
301 / 886-2141

Business Season: April 1 to November 15

Hours: open daily—11 AM to 10 PM

Waterview: Knapps Narrows

Credit Cards: Visa, MasterCard, American Express

House Specialties: oysters creole, crab meat cocktail, sherried crab bisque, scampi with linguini, stuffed oysters mornay, crab cakes, stuffed soft crabs, scallops fettucini, crab imperial, grilled swordfish

During the War of 1812, the British captured and held Tilghman Island as a supply base. Long before that, the Choptank Indians claimed the island. Today on the island, seafood is the county's most important product. So seek out the Tilghman Inn.

The restaurant overlooks the dock, the narrows, and the marsh beyond. A spacious dining room shares the view with an outdoor patio deck. Both offer guests delightful food with a panoramic setting.

For openers, try clams or oyster creole wrapped in bacon and broiled with a spicy sauce. The crab meat cocktail is excellent, and the sherried crab bisque or oyster stew superb. All entrees are served with home-baked bread and the freshest vegetables available. Salads include mixed green, caesar, or spinach leaf. Entrees are many, so I'll just mention a few of my favorites. The grilled Atlantic swordfish is topped with a special compound butter. The scallops fettucini are plump, tender ocean scallops sauteed in white wine sauce, served on a bed of fettucini, and topped with freshly grated parmesan cheese.

HARRISON'S CHESAPEAKE HOUSE

Route 33
Tilghman Island, Maryland
301 / 886-2123

Business Season: all year

Hours: open daily—6 AM to 9:30 PM

Waterview: Choptank River

Credit Cards: MasterCard and Visa

House Specialties: oyster cocktail, oysters on the half shell, shrimp cocktail, oyster stew, cream of crab soup, Maryland crab soup, crab imperial, fried chicken, crab cake, backfin crab meat au gratin, broiled flounder, stuffed shrimp, scallops au gratin, crab and shrimp Norfolk

As you cross the causeway, you enter Tilghman Island, surrounded by the Choptank River which, at the tip, joins the Chesapeake Bay. The island is almost completely made of oyster shells thrown overboard by the shucking houses that were originally on piers built over the water. Depending on the season, you can enjoy watching boats such as "skipjacks" coming into harbor or crab boats delivering their catch to the community docks.

Harrison's is a sprawling country inn and sports fishing center with a fleet of 14 charter fishing boats. The lodging facilities have porch swings. The oldest part of the inn was built in 1856. The three waterfront dining rooms offer southern cuisine created by the Harrison family for over three generations. Enjoy meals such as fried chicken and crab cakes with fresh vegetables and homemade bread. Or try the great soft shell crab sandwich or the oyster buffet which includes oysters served eight ways.

TOWN CREEK RESTAURANT
Tilghman Street
Oxford, Maryland
301 / 226-5131

Business Season: all year

Hours: Tuesday through Sunday—11:30 AM to 10 PM, closed Monday

Waterview: Town Creek / Tred Avon River

Credit Cards: MasterCard and Visa

House Specialties: clams casino, oyster stew, oysters on the half shell, crab cakes, shrimp scampi, crab imperial, soft crab platter, filet of founder, crab soup

The town of Oxford lies on a small peninsula between Town Creek and the Tred Avon River. Fifty years ago, watermen dominated the economy and yachting attracted only the wealthy. Today Oxford is still a watermen's town, but is enjoying a resurgence based on tourism and leisure activities. Its quiet charm, fresh air, summer breezes, boats, weekend visitors, and summer residents offer a welcome change from the hustle and bustle of city life. I like to arrive via the Bellevue, Oxford Ferry, a 20-minute adventure.

The Town Creek Restaurant has expanded attractively in the last few years. Visitors soon learn that this popular restaurant occupies a former crab and oyster packing house. The menu welcomes you with the following: "Our entrees include many seafood dishes prepared from unique eastern shore recipes, and there are a variety of other choices as well. We hope you will enjoy your visit as much as we enjoy having you with us. We invite you to sit back, relax, and enjoy what we like to refer to as...The Oxford Experience."

PIER STREET RESTAURANT
Pier Street
Oxford, Maryland
301 / 226-5171

Business Season: all year

Hours: open daily—11:30 AM to 10 PM

Waterview: Tred Avon River

Credit Cards: Visa and MasterCard

House Specialties: soft crabs, crab cakes, steamed crabs, flounder stuffed with crab meat, steamed oysters, crab au gratin, crab imperial

Oxford, one of the oldest towns in Maryland, was officially founded in 1683, when it was named by the Maryland General Assembly. When we arrived, a worker was cleaning the day's catch at the water's edge. The delicately carved filets were 12 inches long.

At the Pier Street Restaurant, we were disappointed to see a red line deleting the rockfish listing on the menu. But red snapper and flounder filled in for the rockfish. They were stuffed with crab imperial made of fresh backfin crab cooked in white sauce. This crab imperial recipe is one of the finest in all the Bay area. Another selection that brought raves was the crab au gratin.

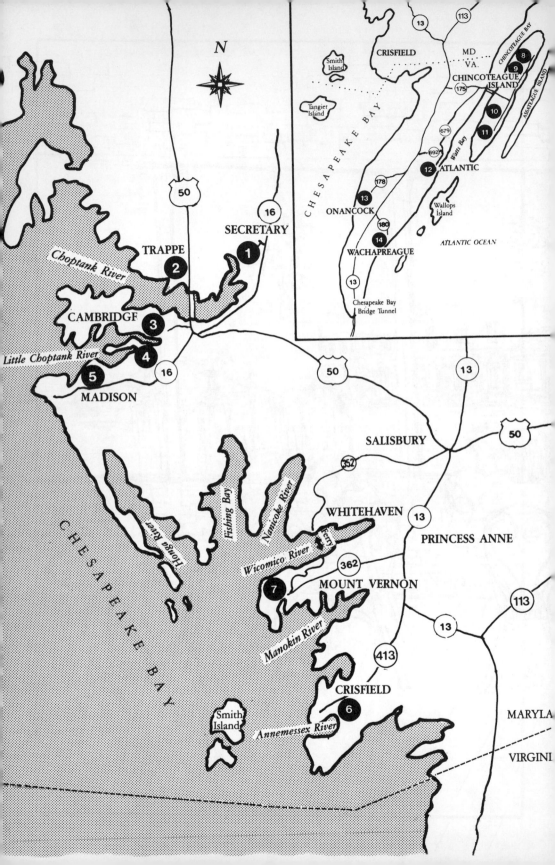

Lower Bay
Waterfront Dining

INCLUDES: Secretary, Trappe, Cambridge, Madison, Crisfield, and Mt. Vernon, Maryland; Chincoteague Island, Atlantic, Onancock, and Wachapreague, Virginia.

1. Suicide Bridge Restaurant
2. Ferry Boat Restaurant
3. Clayton's on the Creek
4. East Side Restaurant
5. Madison Bay Restaurant
6. Captain's Galley Restaurant
7. Harbor Cove
8. Shucking House Cafe
9. Landmark Crab House
10. The Chincoteague Inn
11. Captain Fish's Steaming Wharf
12. Wright's Seafood Restaurant
13. Hopkins & Bro. Store
14. Island House Restaurant

SUICIDE BRIDGE RESTAURANT

Suicide Bridge Road
Secretary, Maryland
301 / 943-4689

Business Season: March 10 to December 27

Hours: Tuesday through Sunday—11 AM to 9 PM, closed Monday

Waterview: Cabin Creek / Choptank River

Credit Cards: none

House Specialties: soft crabs, steamed crabs, crab soup, steamed oysters, oyster stew, clams casino, oysters casino, broiled scallops, clam chowder, surf 'n' turf, crab bisque, crab imperial, crab meat au gratin, catch of the day

Though its specialty is crabs, the kitchen will be happy to steam any of the following for you—shrimp, clams, oysters, scallops, and lobster tails. After you have worked your way through the steam pot, select from the raw bar. If oysters are in season, your visit can't fail.

The menu lists four soups—crab, crab bisque, oyster stew, and clam chowder. Don't skip anything. The selection of baskets and sandwiches is rich in taste and rewarding. Now go to the entrees, which include soft shell crab, crab cake, jumbo shrimp, crab imperial, backfin au gratin, fish (the catch of the day), scallops, oysters, steamed seafood combinations, and lobster tail with delmonico steak.

FERRY BOAT RESTAURANT
Route 50
Trappe, Maryland
301 / 476-3025

Business Season: May 1 through December 1

Hours: Friday through Monday—4 PM to 10 PM

Waterview: Choptank River

Credit Cards: none

House Specialties: all you can eat (steamed crabs, clams, soup and chicken), fried oysters, crab cakes, stuffed flounder, stuffed shrimp

The waters of the Chesapeake Bay were naturally the first roadway known to a settler. To cross the streams that separated him from his neighbor or to transact business, any type of craft was pressed into service—canoes, punts, flatboards, scows, even rafts. The Hampton Roads Ferry Boat Restaurant, built in 1925, was once used to carry as many as 60 automobiles as it traveled from Hampton Roads to Norfolk.

Today the Ferry boat is beached at the foot of the Choptank River Bridge. A large hole was dug on land, and at high tide the boat was pushed to its present location by barge. Downstairs is now a bait and tackle shop and upstairs is the restaurant. Visit yourself, try the all-you-can-eat feast offered by owner Bill Creighton, and see for yourself what a Hampton Roads ferryboat is doing on the Choptank River.

CLAYTON'S ON THE CREEK

112 Commerce Street
Cambridge, Maryland
301 / 228-7200

Business Season: all year

Hours: open daily—11 AM to 10 PM

Waterview: Cambridge Creek / Choptank River

Credit Cards: Visa and MasterCard

House Specialties: crab soup, crab balls, steamed crabs, stuffed potato skins, steamed clams, crab imperial, soft shell crab, crab cakes, seafood platter, baked oysters casserole, fried oysters, seafood kabob, catch of the day

"Is company coming? and you are looking for a place to go?" There is nothing like an open deck at the water's edge on a warm spring day. Clayton's, a restaurant opened by the J.M. Clayton Company in 1985 on the same piece of waterfront that got the family started in the seafood business nearly a century ago, offers fresh seafood bought daily from local watermen. The inside is clean and airy with nautical hues of blue and white, and every seat features a view of the waterfront.

Study the menu. You may choose to begin your dining experience with potato skins stuffed with crab-claw meat and cheese. Now you're ready to order an entree. There are six crab dishes, four shrimp dishes, and additional listings for oysters, clams, and scallops. Your meal will come with hot bread and butter and a choice of two of the following—french fries, baked potato, tossed garden salad, macaroni salad, cole slaw, applesauce, stewed tomatoes, or daily vegetables.

The management advises, "Due to our desire to serve only the freshest seafood, the catch of the day varies. Your server will inform you what is fresh enough to be selected as today's special."

EAST SIDE RESTAURANT

201 Trenton Street
Cambridge, Maryland
301 / 228-9007

Business Season: all year

Hours: Monday through Thursday—4 PM to midnight,
Friday—2 PM to midnight, Saturday and Sunday—11 AM to
1 PM

Waterview: Cambridge Creek / Choptank River

Credit Cards: none

House Specialties: broiled or fried fish of the day, fried oysters,
crab imperial, crab cakes, scallops, soft shell crab, clam chowder,
crab soup

East Side Restaurant is located at the foot of the Cambridge Creek
Bridge. The downstairs room doubles as a steam room for carry-out orders.
Upstairs is where you'll want to be. The bar practically fills the room, but
the mirrored wall gives the illusion of more space. The upstairs outdoor
patio was just about filled with patrons when we arrived but, as luck would
have it, we found a table with a splendid view. The home made crab soup
was full of crab meat, and the clam chowder thick and creamy.

MADISON BAY RESTAURANT

Madison Can House Road
Madison, Maryland
301 / 228-4111

Business Season: all year

Hours: Wednesday through Sunday—11 AM to 10 PM

Waterview: Madison Bay / Little Choptank River

Credit Cards: none

House Specialties: steamed shrimp, breaded oysters, soft crab
sandwich, oyster fritters, crab imperial, fresh fish

When we arrived that day in the middle of June at the Madison Bay
Restaurant, it was hot, and I was hot on the trail of the soft shell crab.
The large parking lot was filled with pick-up trucks. The crab boats were
returning with the day's catch. My waitress arrived promptly with a glass
of refreshing iced tea. Two soft shell crabs, large fat beauties, arrived between
two slices of white bread. On the plate was a plastic container of tartar
sauce. A nearby table quickly filled with local watermen. After lunch, I
paid a visit to nearby Trinity Church—America's oldest church, dating back
to 1675.

CAPTAIN'S GALLEY RESTAURANT
Main Street
Crisfield, Maryland
301 / 968-1636

Business Season: all year

Hours: open daily—breakfast, lunch, and dinner

Waterview: Annemessex River

Credit Cards: Visa and MasterCard

House Specialties: crab cakes, oysters on the half shell, crab meat cocktail, crab soup, she crab soup, clam chowder, oyster stew, oyster fritters, fried oysters, stuffed shrimp, soft shell crabs, fried scallops, crab imperial, crab au gratin

Crisfield, an eastern shore village, is the crab capital of the world, and the Captain's Galley bills itself as "Home of the World's Best Crab Cake." And should you think this is mere exaggeration, realize that this restaurant has been featured in *Southern Living, Good Food, The New York Times, People, Maryland Magazine,* and *Books and People.*

The view from the restaurant is memorable. From your seat you can watch the cruise and mail boats that leave daily to go to Smith and Tangier Island. There is always a hub of excitement with the constant moving of the boats and watermen.

HARBOR COVE
Route 362
Mt. Vernon, Maryland
301 / 651-0552

Business Season: May to December

Hours: open daily—12 noon to 10 PM

Waterview: Wicomico River

Credit Cards: Visa and MasterCard

House Specialties: baked stuffed shrimp, oyster platter, fried shrimp, crab imperial, crab cakes, soft shell crabs

Today many people recognize the soft shell crab as a true delicacy. Soft shell crabs are not a separate species of crab, but are blue crabs that have just molted their hard outer shell in preparation for growth. Once you have cleaned them, you're ready to cook this gourmet delight. The most common preparation technique is either pan fried or deep-fat fried. If you don't want to cook, a good place to taste the soft shell crab is at Harbor Cove.

You enter by way of the screened side porch. Inside are several small wood-panelled rooms. Thick, heavy glass covers the green tablecloths, and green curtains frame the large windows. The soft shell crabs are superb and come served on fresh bread accompanied by a generous portion of cole slaw.

Plan your visit here with a walk around Whitehaven. The ferry that operates here has been in service since about 1692 and is Maryland's only free ferry.

SHUCKING HOUSE CAFE

Main Street
Chincoteague Island, Virginia
804 / 336-5145

Business Season: all year

Hours: open daily—7 AM to 10 PM

Waterview: Chincoteague Bay

Credit Cards: Visa and MasterCard

House Specialties: fried oysters, fried clams, oysters on the half shell, clams on the half shell, cream of crab soup, crab cakes, crab imperial, clam chowder, fish of the day, soft shell crab sandwich

Located in the Landmark Plaza Shopping Center, the Shucking House Cafe offers a splendid view of the boats and trawlers that ply the channel on the Chincoteague Bay. Just aim your car toward the far end of the large gravel parking lot toward the boats. You may sit on the Cafe's large steam deck or inside the restaurant, where it's more festive with pine tables on red and pink carpet, and chairs like ice cream parlor chairs with red seats. There are red place mats and even a red long-stemmed rose on each table (artificial, of course), and plants everywhere.

But a lovely setting is only the beginning. I can attest to the flavor the cook achieved in the oysters and clam strips that were breaded and fried to a golden brown, and served hot and crispy. The soft shell crab sandwich was good and so was the cream of crab soup. I could go on, but come see for yourself. The drive in itself is one you will never forget.

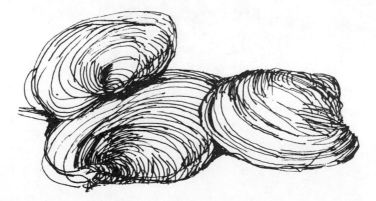

LANDMARK CRAB HOUSE

Main Street
Landmark Plaza
Chincoteague Island, Virginia

Business Season: all year

Hours: Monday through Saturday—5 PM to 9 PM, Sunday—
1 PM to 9 PM, closed Monday in winter

Waterview: Chincoteague Bay

Credit Cards: Visa and MasterCard

House Specialties: Chincoteague oysters, crab Norfolk, crab cakes,
steamed crabs, crab imperial, catch of the day, oyster stew

Old timers like to reflect on the island as it once was when two-masted
ocean-going schooners dotted the channel waters either coming back from
their coastal port calls, or leaving the island loaded with oysters and clams.
Today the waterman and fisherman still remain the chief occupants of the
island. Tourists are next. But whether tourist or waterman, you must visit
the Landmark Crab House and feast on world famous Chincoteague oysters
fresh on the half shell, considered by epicureans worldwide to be the "prince
of the oyster." Try a dozen or so. No other oyster has the taste of a Chincoteague. Include this small fishing village on any trip to the Bay area.

THE CHINCOTEAGUE INN
Marlin Street
Chincoteague Island, Virginia
804 / 336-3314

Business Season: all year

Hours: Sunday through Thursday—11:30 AM to 9 PM, Friday and Saturday—11:30 AM to 10 PM

Waterview: Chincoteague Bay

Credit Cards: Visa and MasterCard

House Specialties: steamed clams, steamed oysters, crab balls, oyster stew, crab soup, flounder almondine, stuffed shrimp, crab imperial, fried oysters, sea trout, broiled scallops, broiled seafood feast

The Chincoteague Island is part of a chain of barrier islands. Shallow bays, marshes, and mud flats separate it from the mainland. Local fishermen help to supply the specials listed on the Chincoteague Inn menu. Here's a sample listing of what the menu has to offer:

"Broiled Seafood Feast:
Scallops, clams, soft crab, fish filet, oysters, stuffed shrimp
Seafood Dream:
A delightful combination of shrimp, scallops and crabmeat broiled in a butter sauce and topped with mozzarella cheese
Famous Fried Combination Seafood:
Fish filet, crab ball, shrimp, scallops, oyster, clam strips"

Nat Kenney, of *National Geographic Magazine*, wrote, "The Inn is a marvelous seafood restaurant." I agree.

CAPTAIN FISH'S STEAMING WHARF

512 South Main Street
Chincoteague Island, Virginia
804 / 336-5997

Business Season: May through September

Hours: Monday through Saturday—11 AM to 9 PM, Sunday—
1 PM to 9 PM

Waterview: Chincoteague Channel

Credit Cards: none

House Specialties: steamed clams, steamed oysters, steamed
mussels, steamed lobster, steamed shrimp, oysters on the half
shell, clams on the half shell, clam chowder

Captain Russell Fish opened his fish company in 1956 and has now
added this restaurant located inside a waterfront pine building. Sit at the
water's edge or inside the new eating pavilion. There are five tables inside
and three outside. The entire menu is seafood freshly steamed to order.
Be sure to inquire about the daily specials.

After dinner, you may choose to take some fresh seafood gathered
daily from Captain Fish's own boats. On my last visit, the offerings included
live lobsters, shrimp, oysters, stone crab claws, soft crabs, steamed crabs,
clams, scallops, and other fish.

WRIGHT'S SEAFOOD RESTAURANT

Atlantic Road
Atlantic, Virginia
804 / 824-4012

Business Season: all year

Hours: Tuesday through Friday—11 AM to 9 PM, Saturday—4 PM to 9 PM, Sunday—12 noon to 9 PM, closed Monday

Waterview: Watts Bay

Credit Cards: American Express, Visa, MasterCard

House Specialties: flounder au gratin, oyster stew, steamed clams, crab balls, baked stuffed shrimp, steamed seafood platter, catch of the day, fried oysters, broiled flounder, crab cakes, crab imperial

If you are lucky enough to be seated at one of this restaurant's large windows, low tide will reveal thousands of sea shells and usually submerged plant life on the shore. Small heron abound here. While you're enjoying the view, treat yourself to one of six seafood appetizers.

For entrees, the menu lists seven different steaks along with fried chicken and pork chops; everything else is seafood—my kind of place. There are 23 seafood entrees to choose from. I'll only mention three—the flounder au gratin stuffed with crab and topped with a cheese sauce; the steamed seafood platter consisting of a small lobster tail, filet of fish, Alaskan crab leg, scallops, steamed shrimp, hard shell clams, and corn on the cob; and Wright's Delight, a variety of seafoods baked in a casserole with imperial sauce.

HOPKINS AND BRO. STORE
2 Market Place
Onancock, Virginia
804 / 787-8220

Business Season: March through December

Hours: open daily—6 AM to 9 PM

Waterview: Onancock Creek

Credit Cards: Visa and MasterCard

House Specialties: steamed clams, catch of the day, seafood salad platter, scallops sauteed in butter, crab Norfolk, crab imperial, crab cakes, soft shell crabs

Onancock's tree lined Main Street with its pleasant homes that display many different architectural styles is perfect for bicycling or walking. It's just a short distance to the wharf, and it is there that you will find the Hopkins and Bro. Store, built in 1842 by Captain Stephen Hopkins.

One of the oldest general stores on the east coast, this family-owned business has spanned four generations. Today it is owned and maintained by the Association for the Preservation of Virginia Antiquities. The store has retained its original charm, and most of the fixtures and equipment are original. You can buy the Spirit of '76 Tangier Cruise tickets from the same ticket window in the store office from which steamboat tickets were sold over a hundred years ago. The trip to Tangier Island that sits in the middle of the Bay is an adventure.

If you miss the boat, don't forget that seafood is featured in the small restaurant where nicely prepared meals are served. Choose from seven appetizers to begin your dining experience. The raw clams can be ordered by the half dozen, and that's a good way to start. Follow up with stuffed flounder or crab cake served with six ounces of delmonico steak. Another good dish is crab Norfolk with Smithfield ham and swiss cheese. Afterwards, shop in the store, which offers a broad variety of general merchandise from groceries to dry goods to quaint arts and crafts.

ISLAND HOUSE RESTAURANT
Main Street
Wachapreague, Virginia
804 / 787-4242

Business Season: March to December

Hours: Monday through Saturday—5:30 PM to 9 PM, Sunday—12 noon to 9 PM

Waterview: Wachapreague Channel / Barrier Islands

Credit Cards: Visa and MasterCard

House Specialties: clam fritters, fish dinner, crab cakes, soft crabs, crab imperial, stuffed flounder, steamed oysters, oysters on the half shell, steamed clams, shrimp cocktail, shrimp scampi

During the early 1900's, the Island House was a hotel and restaurant on Cedar Island. The hotel offered surf bathing that was unsurpassed, with both rough and gentle waves off beautiful sandy beaches. It all washed away during the storm of 1933. The present Island House was constructed after the Hotel Wachapreague burned down in July of 1978.

Today the management still offers clam fritters, a hotel special since 1902. Another local favorite is a brace of quail, in which two farm-raised quail are baked and served over wild rice. All entrees include a trip to the soup and salad boat, fresh bread, baked potato or fries, and vegetable of the day.

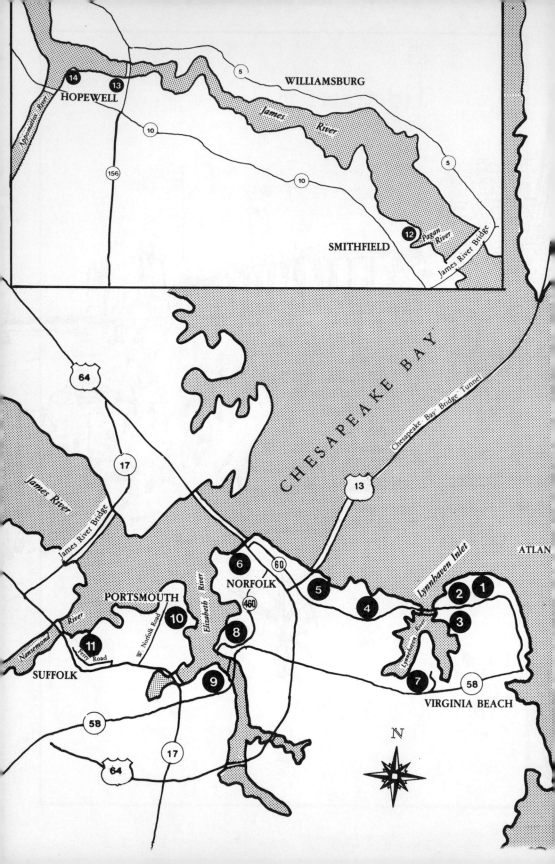

Tidewater
Waterfront Dining

INCLUDES: *Virginia Beach, Norfolk, Portsmouth, Suffolk, Smithfield, and Hopewell, Virginia.*

1. Lynnhaven Fish House
2. Duck—In
3. Henry's
4. The Ship's Cabin
5. Alexander's on the Bay
6. Fisherman's Wharf
7. Steinhilbers—Thalia Acre's Inn
8. Phillips Waterside
9. The Seawall Restaurant
10. Scale O'De Whale
11. Creekside Restaurant
12. Smithfield Station
13. Wheel House Restaurant
14. Navigator's Den

LYNNHAVEN FISH HOUSE
2350 Starfish Road
Virginia Beach, Virginia
804 / 481-0003

Business Season: all year

Hours: Sunday through Thursday—11:30 AM to 10:30 PM, Friday and Saturday—11:30 AM to 11 PM

Waterview: Chesapeake Bay

Credit Cards: MasterCard, Visa, American Express, Choice

House Specialties: oysters on the half shell, clams on the half shell, baked mussels, crab cocktail, crab soup, steamed shrimp, clam chowder, she crab soup, seafood salad, baked stuffed flounder, mariner's platter, crab cakes, soft shell crabs, catch of the day

The menu tells the story:

"As early as colonial times, man had a dream of connecting Virginia's Eastern Shore with the mainland. The dream became a reality on April 15, 1964, when the Chesapeake Bay Bridge-Tunnel was opened to the public, after 3 1/2 years of construction. In 1965, the Bridge-Tunnel was recognized as 'the Outstanding Civil Engineering Achievement' and is acclaimed worldwide as one of the 'seven wonders of the modern world.'

"Known today as the world's largest bridge-tunnel, the facility measures 17.6 miles (28.4 km.) from shore to shore (23 miles total length). To complete the project required twelve miles of trestled roadway; two mile-long tunnels; two bridges; nearly two miles of causeway; four man-made islands; 34,000 carloads of rock to armor the islands; and 5 1/2 miles of approach roads.

"A total of $200 million was spent to complete the Chesapeake Bay Bridge-Tunnel.

"The Bridge-Tunnel is the link to U.S. Highway 13, offering the fastest and most direct route between southeastern Virginia and the Delmarva Peninsula.

"Our story is simply stated at the LYNNHAVEN FISH HOUSE: 'We hope to have filled your glass to the rim, your dish with delight...and all of your expectations.' "

DUCK-IN

3324 Shore Drive
Virginia Beach, Virginia
804 / 481-0201

Business Season: all year

Hours: open daily—breakfast, lunch, dinner

Waterview: Chesapeake Bay

Credit Cards: MasterCard, Visa, American Express

House Specialties: broiled seafood dinner, oysters on the half shell, steamed oysters, oyster stew, steamed clams, crab cakes, broiled stuffed flounder, broiled trout, fisherman's chowder

The menu tells the history of this restaurant with the charming name:
"Duck-In has grown slowly and naturally over the past thirty plus years. Our most recent renovation and expansion, which occured during the spring and summer of 1982, was the fourth. Duck-In began as a small roadside diner and carry-out store right on the shoulder of Shore Drive, next to the old Lesner Bridge and train trestle, in 1952.

"The old building was saved from demolition when W.R. Miller, Jr., successfully petitioned the State of Virginia to move the building northeastward to make way for the new concrete bridges. He had the 'new' Duck-In placed atop pilings at the water's edge and added a porch for dining.

"Duck-In is a regular stopping place for every segment of our community and beyond. Tourists, watermen, families, workers, businessmen, and professionals can count on finding a constant, friendly reception when they walk through our door. Friends, neighbors, loyal customers and Duck-In's Coffee Club members have contributed recipes and suggestions over the years.

"Our weather station in the lobby is used by watermen, sailors and sport fishermen to check water and weather conditions before setting out for work or play.

"It is appropriate that Duck-In sits overlooking the mouth of the Chesapeake Bay, since the lower Bay and the salt marshes of Virginia's Eastern Shore provide most of our fare and are the source of the largest seafood industry in the United States."

HENRY'S
3319 Shore Drive
Virginia Beach, Virginia
804 / 481-7300

Business Season: all year

Hours: open daily—11 AM to 2 PM

Waterview: Lynnhaven Bay

Credit Cards: Visa, MasterCard, American Express

House Specialties: crab meat cocktail, clam chowder, she crab soup, oyster stew, oysters on the half shell, clams on the half shell, fried oysters, crab cakes, steamed seafood platter, cold seafood platter, fish of the day, crab meat in hot butter, soft shell crabs, clam fritters, crab meat salad

Outside Henry's, you can watch the boats coming through the inlet and the waves breaking on the jetties. Inside, listen to the watermen seated at the tables talk of the day's catch. Everyone is polite and very friendly.

If you are a true seafood lover, go for the steamed seafood platter for two. It contains clams, oysters, shrimp, poached fish, scallops, crab meat, corn on the cob, and potatoes. This meal, available only after 5 PM, takes 20-25 minutes to cook. Most seafood on the menu can be fried or broiled, and don't worry—the waiters won't forget the hush puppies.

THE SHIP'S CABIN

4110 East Ocean View Avenue
Virginia Beach, Virginia
804 / 480-2526

Business Season: all year

Hours: Monday, Wednesday through Friday—lunch 11:30 AM to 3 PM, dinner 5 PM to 10 PM; Saturday and Sunday—11:30 AM to 10 PM; closed Tuesday

Waterview: Chesapeake Bay

Credit Cards: Choice, MasterCard, Visa, Diners Club, American Express

House Specialties: crab cakes, broiled scallops, oysters on the half shell, oyster stew, fresh fish of the day, she crab soup, flounder stuffed with crab meat, crab Norfolk, soft shell crab, oysters bingo, baked shrimp, seafood kabob

The menu says it best: "One of the leading business publications in the country, *Sales and Marketing Management Magazine,* lists the Ships Cabin among the top 100 restaurants in North America. It has earned a five star rating from *Commonwealth Magazine* and rates three stars from the prestigious *Mobile Travel Guide.* It won both best restaurant and best seafood restaurant honors in *Port Folio,* and has been recognized by *Gourmet, Cuisine,* and *Bon Appetit....*

"The interior does indeed resemble a ship's cabin, with dark wood paneled walls, ceiling fans, brass lamps, and exposed timber. The bayside dining room is the perfect showcase for some of the best seafood in the world...."

The menu varies depending on what is in season. "A single evening may offer two dozen seafood entrees, ranging from perhaps a simple, excellent baked shrimp and crab in cheese to a tender delicate hardwood grilled seafood kebab." But oysters bingo, the restaurant's specialty, is always available. In this dish, fresh oysters are lightly floured and sauteed, placed on heated shells, and then covered with a wine sauce containing shallots and lemon juice. Nothing is deep fat fried here. Fresh vegetables are steamed. The menu also offers steak, veal, and chicken, and more than a hundred of the finest wines.

ALEXANDER'S ON THE BAY

4536 Ocean View Avenue
Virginia Beach, Virginia
804 / 464-4999

Business Season: all year

Hours: open daily—5 PM to 10:30 PM

Waterview: Chesapeake Bay

Credit Cards: MasterCard, Visa, Choice, American Express

House Specialties: filet of flounder, broiled seafood combination platter, crab cakes, soft shell crabs, crab meat au gratin, seafood brochette, oysters Rockefeller, oysters on the half shell, clams on the half shell, shrimp and asparagus bisque, filet of flounder stuffed with crab imperial, fried oysters

Alexander's on the Bay is located at the foot of Fentress Street near the Chesapeake Bay Bridge-Tunnel. The blue awnings outside set the tone for pastel grey walls inside. The dining room has a gracious yet relaxed atmosphere, the cuisine is superb yet unpretentious, the tables, glassware, and silverware spotless, and fresh flowers adorn every table.

There are 11 seafood appetizers and 15 seafood entrees. All breads are fresh baked on the premises. Enjoy your dinner and the extraordinary view of the Bay.

FISHERMAN'S WHARF

1571 West Ocean View Avenue
Norfolk, Virginia
804 / 480-3113

Business Season: all year

Hours: open daily—6 AM to 11 PM

Waterview: Hampton Creek / Hampton Roads Harbor

Credit Cards: MasterCard, Visa, American Express, Carte Blanche, Diners Club

House Specialties: lump crab meat cocktail, oysters on the half shell, stuffed mushrooms imperial, baked imperial crab, stuffed filet of flounder, crab meat au gratin, seafood shish-kabob, seafood platter

There are actually two Fisherman's Wharf Restaurants—one across the Hampton Roads harbor in Hampton and one in Norfolk. Like its namesake, the Norfolk restaurant serves one of the largest and finest seafood buffets on the east coast. Another feature is Blackbeard's Feast, a spirited name for what is commonly called Surf and Turf—filet mignon and lobster tail.

The Tidewater area may be the east coast's best kept secret, located on the confluence where the Atlantic Ocean flows with the mighty Chesapeake Bay, it's a low-lying coastal plain of southeastern Virginia. Seven cities are at the water's edge. The towns and cities are split by rivers, streams, canals, and creeks. The locals may live in different cities, or work in different cities, but they all dine at the Fisherman's Wharf.

STEINHILBER'S—
THALIA ACRES INN
653 Thalia Road North
Virginia Beach, Virginia
804 / 340-1156

Business Season: all year

Hours: Tuesday through Saturday—5 PM to 10 PM

Waterview: Western Branch, Lynnhaven River

Credit Cards: Visa and MasterCard

House Specialties: fried shrimp, clams on the half shell, oysters on the half shell, shrimp cocktail, crab meat cocktail, clam chowder, seafood chowder, crab meat in butter sauce, imperial crab, seafood platter, fried oysters, stuffed flounder, grilled swordfish, seafood combination platter

The menu gives this brief history of the restaurant:

"In 1932, Robert Steinhilber decided to get away from the restaurant business and Norfolk's 'city life' and moved to the country. In 1935 he purchased the site of the Lynnhaven Golf and Country Club on the Lynnhaven River.

"Thalia Acres as it came to be known, emerged as a weekend retreat offering horseback riding, canoeing and hiking. But friends soon convinced 'Steiny' to open a restaurant. In 1937, building on the original foundation of the clubhouse, he personally began the construction of the present main dining room. In 1939, after marrying Marion Eley, he opened the doors to what has become one of the oldest family owned and operated restaurants in Virginia, Steinhilber's Thalia Acres Inn.

"Working tirelessly for many years in his own unique style, Robert Steinhilber set the standards and began the traditions of fine food, good service and southern hospitality that his restaurant became noted for. His children, Jeanne and Steve, are proud to follow in his footsteps."

PHILLIPS WATERSIDE
333 Waterside Drive
Norfolk, Virginia
804 / 627-6600

Business Season: all year

Hours: Monday through Friday—11 AM to 10 PM, Saturday and Sunday—11 AM to 11:30 PM

Waterview: Elizabeth River

Credit Cards: Visa, MasterCard, Diners Club

House Specialties: clams on the half shell, oysters on the half shell, crab claw cocktail, steamer buckets, crab soup, crab cakes, fresh fish of the day, fried seafood platter, steamed seafood platter, crab imperial, fried oysters, steamed scallops

There's no better place to be than Norfolk by the sea, where a world of wonder awaits you on the waterfront overlooking the bustling Elizabeth River. And Phillips is the place to begin your Chesapeake Bay tradition of fine food. A Victorian theme is established by its Tiffany-style lamps, stained glass windows, and sewing machine tables.

The menu tells of a delicious house specialty, flounder, so come to Phillips for a taste.

"Marketed as 'FLUKE,' Summer Flounder is considered the finest eating of all flatfish in the Flounder family. For this reason, regardless of its higher cost, Fluke is used almost exclusively in our restaurants. Summer Flounder occur in the eastern U.S. from Maine to South Carolina. They are most available in the summer months when they frequent shallow water. During the winter they range in the 150- to 300-foot depths off-shore. The angler's catch often surpasses the commercial catch. Fluke meat is firm, lean, and white."

THE SEAWALL RESTAURANT

425 Water Street
Portsmouth, Virginia
804 / 397-7006

Business Season: all year

Hours: Sunday through Thursday—11:15 AM to 10 PM, Friday and Saturday—11:15 AM to 11 PM

Waterview: Southern Branch, Elizabeth River

Credit Cards: MasterCard, Visa, American Express, Diners Club, Carte Blanche

House Specialties: clams casino, shrimp scampi, clam chowder, crab cakes, steamed shrimp, fried oysters, seafood platter, seafood salad, fresh filet stuffed with crab meat

The menu tells the story:

"The principles of restaurant hospitality. . .though most often forgotten. . .consist simply of good food, attentive service, and pleasant atmosphere. At The Seawall, however, we strive to provide excellent food, superb service, and great atmosphere. The spectacular view from The Seawall is just one more plus for our very special guests.

"Our standards are high and we are determined to maintain them. After all, the quality of our restaurant is reflected in the quality of our customers. . .and of that we are most proud.

"We thank you for your support and your patronage. . .and we pledge an ongoing effort to continue to deserve both."

The Seawall is located across the Elizabeth River from the Waterside, next to the pedestrian ferry dock. Come by ferry or car and feast on fresh seafood specialties. Or choose prime rib, sandwiches, or salad bar, or the special Sunday brunch. Relax with cocktails by the fireplace or on the riverside deck while you enjoy the fantastic view of the water and the Norfolk skyline.

An historical marker outside the Seawall sets the scene. "The Elizabeth River, explored by Captain John Smith in 1608, was named for Princess Elizabeth. Shipbuilding activity began in 1620 when John Wood, a shipbuilder, requested a land grant. Many historic ships were built at the Naval shipyard here including the USS Delaware, the first ship dry-docked in America and CCCS Virginia, Ex-Merrimac, the first ironclad to engage in battle." So visit Jim and Jerry's place on the water.

SCALE O'DE WHALE

3515 Shipwright Street
Portsmouth, Virginia
804 / 483-2772

Business Season: all year

Hours: open daily—Monday through Friday—11:30 AM to 10 PM, Saturday and Sunday—5:30 PM to 10 PM

Waterview: Elizabeth River

Credit Cards: MasterCard, Visa, American Express, Diners Club

House Specialties: oysters hollandaise, oysters Rockefeller, clams casino, scallops with lobster sauce, scallops kabob, seafood platter, crab cakes, soft shell crabs, fried oysters, she crab soup, clam chowder, shrimp cocktail, filet of flounder

Scale O'De Whale is located at the foot of the new West Norfolk Bridge. Built out on a pier at the water's edge, the restaurant serves superb seafood and offers a view of sunset and seagulls.

For starters, you might begin with my favorite, the she crab soup, or try the clam chowder, oysters Rockefeller, shrimp cocktail, clams casino, or oysters hollandaise. Entrees of special note are the broiled or fried seafood platter and the "Islander"—juicy shrimp, scallops, and tender chunks of filet mignon skewered among fresh garden vegetables, lightly glazed in a Hawaiian sauce served on rice pilaf, and accompanied by a tossed salad.

For lunch I had a hard time selecting a sandwich from my three all-time favorites, fried flounder, soft shell crab, and crab cakes. I went finally with the soft shell crab, a seasonal delicacy, and was rewarded with a delicious sandwich.

121

CREEKSIDE RESTAURANT

3305 Ferry Road
Suffolk, Virginia
804 / 484-8700

Business Season: all year

Hours: Tuesday through Thursday—4 PM to 9 PM, Friday and Saturday—4 PM to 10 PM, Sunday—1:30 AM to 10 PM, closed Monday

Waterview: Bennett's Creek / Nansemond River

Credit Cards: Visa, MasterCard, Choice, American Express

House Specialties: soft shell crabs, crab cakes, fish of the day, crab salad, crab cocktail, she crab soup, clam chowder, steamed shrimp, seafood platter, clam strips, broiled seafood combination platter

This restaurant is not for those who want little extras. Its plain, simply done menu matches the plain, white frame building. The main attraction here is the fresh food cooked to your order.

I timed my visit with the soft shell crab season and ordered the house offering. That's where the plainness ended, and good food and good service began. The soft shell crab was cooked to perfection, golden brown and juicy. It came with sliced tomatoes, golden french fries, coleslaw, and hush puppies. It was so good, in fact, that I ordered another to go, for the long journey home.

To reach Creekside, travel south on Route 17. After crossing the Nansemond River Bridge, turn left onto Knott's Neck Road, take another left onto Ferry Road, and follow it to the end.

SMITHFIELD STATION

415 South Church Street
Smithfield, Virginia
804 / 357-7700

Business Season: all year

Hours: open daily—breakfast, lunch, and dinner

Waterview: Cypress Creek / Pagan River

Credit Cards: Visa, MasterCard, Choice, American Express

House Specialties: fresh shucked oysters or clams, shrimp or crab meat cocktail, crab soup, shrimp and crab meat salad, steamed mussels, clams or oysters, baked shrimp, oysters en casserole, crab imperial, crab Norfolk, crab cakes, stuffed flounder, fried spot, seafood platter

While you are visiting this tiny tidewater town, take a walking tour of the 30 historic building sites located just blocks from Smithfield Station. Included in this tour are buildings dating from the 18th century to pre-Civil War times. In nearby Surry County, a stop at Bacon's Castle is a real treat. Built in 1665, it is the oldest documented house in North America. Smith's Fort Plantation, also in Surry County, is an interesting step back in time. The land was given by Chief Powhatan to John Rolfe on the occasion of his marriage to Pocahontas in 1614.

Your appetite now inspired by early American history, head on back to Smithfield Station and enjoy what this part of the Bay is all about—good home cookin'. The restaurant, designed to complement the old Victorian homes down the street, sits on a site at the foot of the bridge crossing Cypress Creek. Its owner, Ron Pack, selected this Pagan River location that also includes a marina and a hotel with 15 guest rooms.

I have several favorite dishes. The seafood platter is a combination of shrimp, oysters, scallops, flounder, and crab cake. It is served either broiled or fried. Seafood rarebit is pan-sauteed and served in a deep-dish cheese melt. A real treat is fried spot—local spot, dressed and lightly floured and deep fried. And then there's the Smithfield ham—I could go on.

WHEELHOUSE RESTAURANT

700 Jordan Point Road
Hopewell, Virginia
804 / 541-2600

Business Season: all year

Hours: Monday through Thursday—4:30 PM to 9 PM, Friday
and Saturday—4:30 PM to 10 PM, Sunday—10:30 AM to 9 PM

Waterview: James River

Credit Cards: Visa and MasterCard

House Specialties: fried oysters, broiled scallops, fried clam strips,
filet of flounder, backfin crab meat au gratin, baked stuffed
shrimp, oysters on the half shell, oysters Rockefeller, steamed clams

This lovely cedar building built in the round is the work of owner
Frank Blaha, Jr. A meal to try is the "Wheelhouse Special" consisting
of shrimp and lobster, crab meat, and wild rice sauteed in garlic butter
with salad or vegetable of the day. On display in the Wheelhouse are many
arrowheads found while pouring the foundation for the restaurant.

Located in Prince George County, Hopewell includes some of the
earliest settled land in Virginia. Lord Cornwallis passed by here in 1781,
pursuing Lafayette. Part of Grant's army passed by on the way to Petersburg
in 1864. At Jordan's Point, 5 miles north on the James River, lived the
Revolutionary leader, Richard Bland, and nearby the great agriculturist,
Edmund Ruffin.

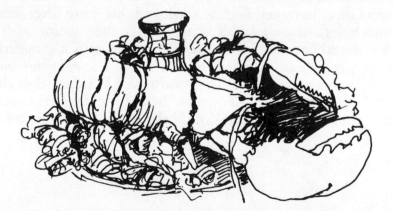

NAVIGATOR'S DEN
Randolph Road (Route 10)
Hopewell, Virginia
804 / 458-9100

Business Season: all year

Hours: Tuesday through Saturday—5 PM to 10 PM, Sunday—12 noon to 9 PM, closed Monday

Waterview: Appomattox River

Credit Cards: Visa and MasterCard

House Specialties: clam chowder, crab meat salad bowl, backfin crab meat cocktail, broiled seafood platter, soft shell crab, broiled scallops, fried oysters, crab cakes, filet of flounder

Just above the point where the Appomattox meets the James River is Shirley Plantation, offering a panorama of rare historical continuity. Shirley was founded 6 years after the settlers arrived at Jamestown in 1607 to establish the first permanent English colony in the New World. Today the historic estate provides an intimate glimpse of a way of life spanning 3 centuries. There are a number of superb brick outbuildings. Of particular interest is the plantation kitchen where many a fine meal was prepared during the 18th and 19th centuries.

Another fine kitchen is that of the Navigator's Den, where the food is first rate. A splendid way to begin your visit is with a backfin crab meat cocktail. Or try the shrimp salad bowl. Seafood entrees outnumber meat dishes; I'll mention a few. There are broiled scallops, fried soft shell clams, broiled backfin crab meat au gratin, or jumbo Virginia soft crabs. If you prefer fish, choose from stuffed baby flounder broiled to perfection or a filet of flounder, fried a rich golden brown. All dinners include salad bar and baked potato, french fries, or vegetable of the day. Bon appetit!

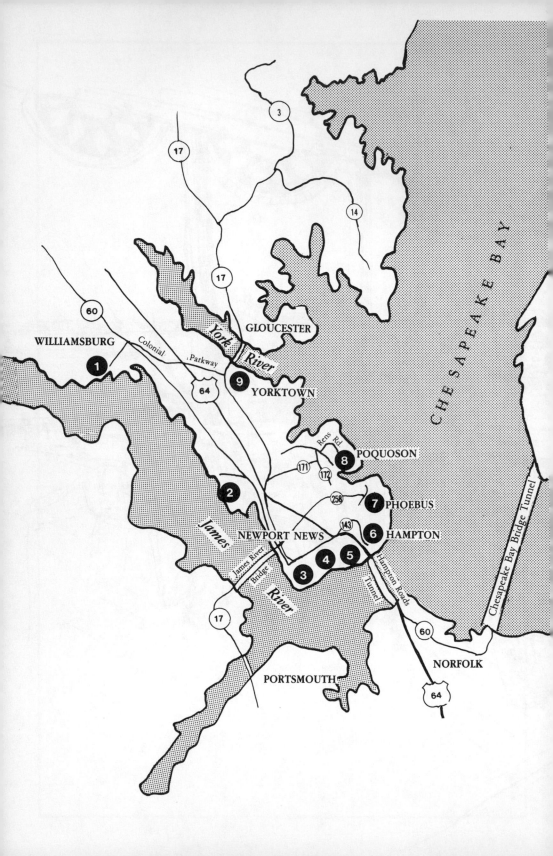

Virginia Peninsula
Waterfront Dining

INCLUDES: Williamsburg, Newport News, Hampton, Phoebus, Poquoson, and Yorktown, Virginia.

1. Kingsmill Restaurant
2. Herman's Harbor House
3. Wharton's Wharf Seafood House
4. Fisherman's Wharf
5. Strawberry Banks Restaurant
6. Chamberlin Hotel Restaurant
7. Sam's Seafood Restaurant
8. The Ship's Galley Restaurant
9. Nick's Seafood Pavilion

KINGSMILL RESTAURANT
100 Kingsmill Road
Williamsburg, Virginia
804 / 253-1703

Business Season: all year

Hours: open daily, Sunday brunch—10 AM to 3 PM

Waterview: James River

Credit Cards: MasterCard, Visa, American Express

House Specialties: crab cakes, fresh yellow tail tuna, fresh Norwegian salmon, soft shell crab, blue crab with American caviar, fried shrimp

Overlooking the James River, Kingsmill, home of the $600,000 Anheuser-Busch Golf Classic on the PGA tour, offers a wealth of beauty and historic tradition. The erosion of a James River bank in 1972 revealed a secret that had been hidden for more than 250 years—a 17th century well shaft. The well and the artifacts recovered from it led to 3 years of extensive research. A sampling of the results is on view at the Kingsmill Restaurant in the foyer to the Riverview Room. Displays include colonial wine bottles and coarse earthenware.

The Kingsmill Restaurant offers superb cuisine served in contemporary surroundings. Here you can dine overlooking the fairways and the river. Enjoy the fresh seafood and the outstanding house specialties with tableside service in the continental tradition.

HERMAN'S HARBOR HOUSE

663 Deep Creek Road
Newport News, Virginia
804 / 930-1000

Business Season: all year

Hours: Monday through Friday—lunch 11:30 AM to 2:30 PM, dinner 5 PM to 10 PM; Saturda—dinner 5 PM to 10 PM; Sunday—11:30 AM to 10 PM

Waterview: Deep Creek / James River

Credit Cards: MasterCard, Visa, American Express

House Specialties: oysters on the half shell, clams on the half shell, she crab soup, clam chowder, seafood chowder, crab cakes, fried oysters, soft shell crabs, imperial crab, shrimp / scallop / or crab meat au gratin, stuffed shrimp, Captain Wyndham's gourmet platter

Herman cautions that Captain Wyndham's Gourmet Platter is only for the very hungry seafood lover. You begin with a cup of fresh salad and oysters and clams on the half shell. Add to that servings of rock lobster, crab imperial, gulf shrimp, sea scallops, and filet of flounder, and you'll see why.

All seafood is carefully selected by Herman whose family has a century of seafood harvesting and processing behind them. Every effort is made to serve the freshest seafood possible prepared to your order.

WHARTON'S WHARF SEAFOOD HOUSE
915 Jefferson Avenue
Newport News, Virginia
804 / 380-1114

Business Season: all year

Hours: open daily May through October—6 AM to 10 PM, winter hours—11 AM to 4 PM

Waterview: Newport News Creek

Credit Cards: Visa, MasterCard, Choice

House Specialties: fish of the day, soft shell crabs, crab meat cold plate, fried shrimp, crab cake dinner, fried or broiled scallops, fried oysters, fried clam strips, clam chowder, shrimp chowder, oyster stew

Wharton's Wharf is home of the Harbor Cruise, featuring both the Newport News shipyard and the Norfolk Naval Base as well as the Merrimac and Monitor sites. The tiny front dining room has pine-paneled walls trimmed in blue and overlooks the harbor cruise boats leaving out of Newport News Creek, making Wharton's a popular dining spot.

Enjoy a delightful lunch or dinner featuring North Atlantic and Chesapeake Bay seafood "fresh from the trawler" and prepared using recipes from local Virginia farmers.

FISHERMAN'S WHARF
14 Ivy Home Road
Hampton, Virginia
804 / 723-3113

Business Season: all year

Hours: Monday through Thursday—5 PM to 10 PM, Friday—5 PM to 10:30 PM, Saturday and Sunday—12 noon to 9 PM

Waterview: Hampton Creek / Hampton Roads Harbor

Credit Cards: MasterCard, Visa, American Express

House Specialties: crab meat cocktail, clams on the half shell, oysters on the half shell, clams casino, oysters Rockefeller, shrimp scampi, broiled seafood platter, seafood buffet, crab cakes, fried clam strips, catch of the day, backfin crab meat saute

For seafood lovers, the seafood buffet offered at Fisherman's Wharf is one of the best the Chesapeake Bay area has to offer. Here's the listing: steamed shrimp, jumbo snow crab legs, shrimp creole, broiled scallops, fried deep sea flounder, fried select oysters, gulf fried shrimp, broiled fish, seafood au gratin, fried ocean clams, imperial crab supreme, baked whole fish, deviled crab, steamed blue crabs, New England clam chowder, fresh salads, breads, vegetables, and desserts—all this and a view of Hampton Roads Harbor filled with ships. The harbor was built in 1610 and is now Virginia's main seafood packing center. All varieties of commercial fishermen work the lower Bay and ocean waters.

To get there from Interstate 64, take LaSalle Avenue and exit to Kecoughtan Road. Turn left on Kecoughtan Road to Ivy Home Road, turn right, and continue to the end of the street.

133

STRAWBERRY BANKS RESTAURANT

Strawberry Banks Lane
Hampton, Virginia
804 / 723-6061

Business Season: all year

Hours: Monday through Saturday—6 AM to 10 PM, Sunday brunch—11 AM to 3 PM

Waterview: Hampton Roads Harbor

Credit Cards: MasterCard, Diners Club, American Express

House Specialties: seafood esplanade, shrimp, crab meat or scallops au gratin, crab meat Norfolk, clam chowder, seafood cocktail, seafood Norfolk, crab cakes, shrimp flambe, broiled scallops, clam chowder, seafood cocktail

Located at Exit 69 off Interstate 64 at the northern approach to Hampton Roads Tunnel, the Strawberry Banks Restaurant offers items such as seafood esplanade, and oysters, shrimp, and scallops broiled and fried. The sound of passing ships, the soft breezes, and the night lights will make every meal unique and wonderful. There's a lot you can do without ever leaving the grounds. You can swim in the fresh-water pool, jog or stroll along a private beach, go fishing, hunt for seashells, or eat at the restaurant.

Here's some historic information provided by the menu:

"According to legend Strawberry Banks witnessed our founding fathers arrival. Captain John Smith was greeted by friendly Kecoughtan Indians from our banks as he and his English settlers sailed towards Jamestown in 1607.

"The Captain noticed the abundance of wild berries on the shore and called this spot 'Strawberry Bankes'."

"From the narrative of Captain George Pearce, one of the 104 first settlers of Virginia:

April 26-29, 1607;

"The six and twentieth day of Aprill, about foure o'clock in the morning, wee descried the land of Virginia...The same day wee entred the Bay of Chesupioc directly, without let or hinderance. There wee landed and discovered a little way, but wee could find nothing worth the speaking of but faire meddowes and goodly fall trees, with such Freshwaters running through the woods that I was almost ravished at the first sight thereof. Going a little further wee came into a little plat of ground full of fine and beautiful strawberries, four times bigger and better than ours in England.''

and

"From land deed of 1637 to Captain Francis Hook:

"A trail of land situated upon the Strawberrie Banckes called by the name Fort Field..."

and

During the Civil War the Battle of the Merrimac and the Monitor took place within view of this same spot.

CHAMBERLIN HOTEL RESTAURANT

Old Point Comfort
Hampton, Virginia
804 / 722-3636

Business Season: all year

Hours: Monday through Thursday—6 PM to 8 PM, Friday and Saturday—6 PM to 9 PM, Sunday brunch—11 AM to 7 PM

Waterview: Chesapeake Bay

Credit Cards: MasterCard, Visa, American Express, Diners Club, Choice

House Specialties: crab bisque, clam chowder, crab Norfolk, stuffed flounder, crab cakes, coconut shrimp, seafood combination platter

For the last half century the Chamberlin has reigned over the majestic waters of the Chesapeake Bay. Today it is a Bay landmark that is still flourishing. The hotel is a full-service conference center and resort offering entertainment and lodging. From your restaurant table, you can look out through the large windows and see all types of boats from a trawler to a tanker located on Fort Monroe at Old Point Comfort. On Friday nights the seafood buffet is as bountiful a gift from the sea as you will ever see.

The Inn also has a formal restaurant, the Great Gatsby, which "captures the carefree, luxurious spirit and romantic ambience of the post-War 1920's. Enjoy breakfast and luncheon buffets, along with candlelight dining." In the Great Gatsby, even Sundays are special with Daisy's champagne brunch.

SAM'S SEAFOOD RESTAURANT

23 Water Street
Phoebus, Virginia
804 / 723-3709

Business Season: all year

Hours: Sunday through Friday—11:30 AM to 10 PM, Saturday—11:30 AM to 11 PM

Waterview: Mill Creek

Credit Cards: MasterCard, American Express, Visa

House Specialties: crab meat cocktail, oyster cocktail, steamed clams, steamed oysters, fried oysters, fried clams, crab cakes, imperial crab, crab meat au gratin, broiled shrimp and crab meat

Exploring the Virginia peninsula with its quaint fishing docks, marshes, and back creeks is an experience well worth the trip. Phoebus is a city of scenic beauty and home port for many fishing boats that sail each day, catching oysters, clams, crabs, and fresh fish. Gourmets consider Chesapeake Bay oysters and crabs to be the best in the world. So while you're vacationing in Phoebus, why not let your adventure begin at Sam's where the seafood is plentiful, the service swift, and prices reasonable. The meal may turn out to be one of your favorite experiences.

Entrees include seafood fried, broiled, in sauce, or sauteed. I especially enjoyed the broiled flounder. Or try a steak served one of three ways. As I sat enjoying my meal, I watched the warm sun play across the river, creating brilliant sparkles on the water.

THE SHIPS GALLEY RESTAURANT
105 Rens Road
Poquoson, Virginia
804 / 868-7980

Business Season: all year

Hours: open daily—6 AM to 10 PM

Waterview: White House Cove / Poquoson River

Credit Cards: Visa and MasterCard

House Specialties: seafood platter, seafood smorgasboard, steamed clams, steamed scallops, steamed shrimp, soft crabs, fried oysters, fried calm strips, crab cakes, oyster sandwich, clam chowder

The menu tells about this interesting history of the city of Poquoson (pronounced Po-ko-son). "Believed to be an ancient Indian word meaning 'low flat land,' the name is applied both to the city and the river on its northern boundary. Two recent archeological digs off Pasture and Brown's Neck Roads uncovered evidence of dwellings prior to 1700. Augustine Warner, forebear of both Queen Elizabeth II and George Washington, owned land near Roberts Creek in 1635 near the intersection of Moore and Wagner Roads. Samuel Bennett owned land on the present Brown's Neck Road which bordered the creek bearing his name in 1636. Artifacts from both sites are on display at the Poquoson Public Library. The Warner site gave evidence of an affluent household."

Try the restaurant's steamed clams, steamed scallops, steamed shrimp, soft crabs, fried oysters, fried clam strips, crab cakes, or oyster sandwich. Or enjoy a hearty bowl of clam chowder.

NICK'S SEAFOOD PAVILION

Water Street
Yorktown, Virginia
804 / 887-5269

Business Season: all year

Hours: open daily—11 AM to 10 PM

Waterview: York River

Credit Cards: MasterCard, Visa, Diners Club, American Express, Choice

House Specialties: clam chowder, turtle au sherry, broiled halibut, filet of fluke, broiled blue fish, combination seafood au gratin, soft shell crabs, crab meat au gratin, crab cakes, oysters on the half shell, clams on the half shell

Visit Yorktown and see the historical exhibits of the Watermen's Museum. At the other end of the block you can watch divers excavating the remains of an English ship that sunk during the seige of Yorktown in 1781. Your appetite having been inspired by your historic explorations, proceed to Nick's famous Seafood Pavilion just under the York River Bridge. The entrance to the restaurant is through a Greek garden. There are several large dining rooms. If you want a waterview, then choose the smaller side room. The Greek influence is evident throughout the restaurant with its greenery and Greek statues.

The clam chowder was a mighty good way to start a recent lunch. The soup was rich and spicy and full of some of the finest clams I have had the good fortune to try. Choosing a main dish was a tough decision, but my selection was the soft shell crabs. The two large crabs were sauteed in butter and garnished with fresh parsley. I found out from this simple lunch why Nick's is patronized by epicureans from all over the world.

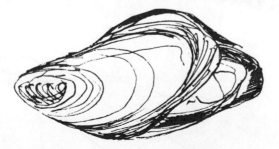

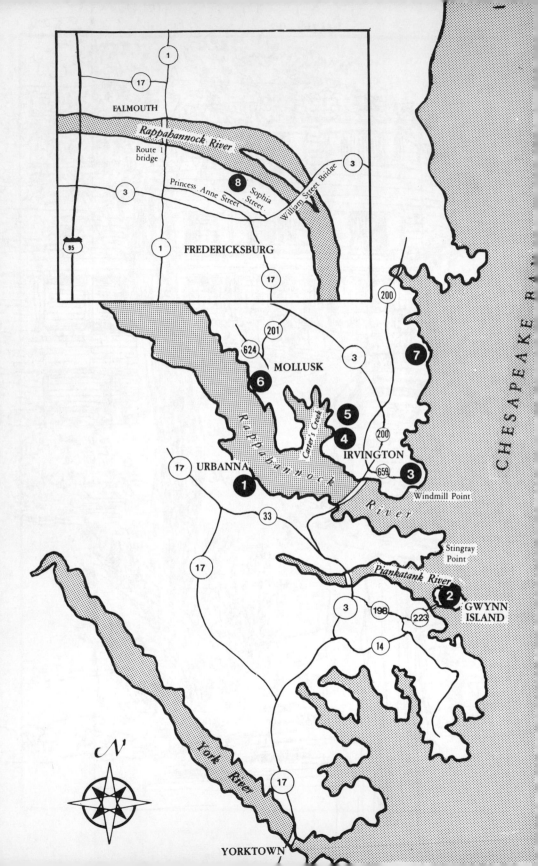

FALMOUTH

Rappahannock River

Route 1 bridge

Princess Anne Street

Sophia Street

William Street Bridge

1

17

3

95

1

FREDERICKSBURG

17

8

3

201

624

MOLLUSK

6

3

200

7

5

4

Carter's Creek

IRVINGTON

200

659

3

17

URBANNA

1

Rappahannock River

Windmill Point

33

17

Stingray Point

Piankatank River

2

GWYNN ISLAND

3

198

223

14

York River

17

YORKTOWN

CHESAPEAKE BAY

N

Middle Peninsula
Waterfront Dining

INCLUDES: Urbanna, Gwynn's Island, Windmill Point, Irvington, Mollusk, Burgess, and Fredericksburg, Virginia.

1. Windows on Urbanna Creek
2. Golden Anchor Restaurant
3. The Dockside Hearth
4. The Tides Inn
5. The Tides Lodge
6. The Upper Deck Restaurant
7. Horn Harbor House
8. Arbuckles

WINDOWS ON URBANNA CREEK
Virginia Street
Urbanna, Virginia
804 / 758-2397

Business Season: all year

Hours: Monday through Saturday—lunch 11:30 AM to 2:30 PM, dinner 5:30 PM to 9 PM; Sunday—11:30 AM to 8 PM

Waterview: Urbanna Creek / Rappahannock River

Credit Cards: MasterCard and Visa

House Specialties: catch of the day, crab cakes, stuffed flounder, oysters on the half shell, oyster stew, fried oysters, crab imperial

Urbanna, on the south shore of the Rappahannock River, was once a port-of-call for the steamboats and sailing ships on the Chesapeake Bay. Today it is home of the annual oyster festival, held the first weekend in November. For 3 days, the town is one big party with oysters sold on nearly every doorstep in town. The rest of the year, the place to go for oysters is the Windows restaurant.

Its location on a creek just off the Bay is well protected, making it an ideal spot for a romantic dockside dining experience. Our view was enhanced by several school girls feeding the many gulls that flocked at the water's edge. My selection, an excellent flounder, was topped with a heavenly cream sauce. The mushroom quiche was fabulous. We sent our compliments to the chef and promised to return.

GOLDEN ANCHOR RESTAURANT
Ferry Road
Gwynn's Island, Virginia
804 / 725-2151

Business Season: April through December

Hours: open daily—breakfast 8 AM to 10 AM , lunch 12 noon to 2 PM, dinner 5 PM to 9 PM; Saturday—dinner till 9:30 PM

Waterview: Piankatank River

Credit Cards: MasterCard and Visa

House Specialties: baked stuffed shrimp, captain's seafood platter, crab cakes, stuffed flounder, imperial crab, fried shrimp

It was here on tiny Gwynn's Island that a grave was dug for Captain John Smith when he was near death following an encounter with a sting ray in the nearby waters. Today, the Islander Motel, one of the Chesapeake Bay's great vacation and conference centers, is located at Narrows Marina. When here, you can dine at the motel's Golden Anchor Restaurant where specialties include seafood from the local waters.

THE DOCKSIDE HEARTH
Route 659
Windmill Point, Virginia
804 / 435-1166

Business Season: March to the first week in January

Hours: open daily—breakfast and lunch 8 AM to 3 PM, dinner 5 PM to 9 PM; Saturday and Sunday—dinner till 10 PM

Waterview: Rappahannock River / Chesapeake Bay

Credit Cards: Visa, MasterCard, American Express, Diners Club

House Specialties: shrimp and crab meat Norfolk, stuffed flounder, crab imperial, seafood bisque, shrimp cocktail, crab cakes, broiled flounder

The menu tells you why you may want to spend several days in this town.

"Located on Virginia's Northern Neck, where the Rappahannock River adjoins the Chesapeake Bay, the Quality Inn Windmill Point Marine Resort delights guests with resort living at its best. Among the many natural attractions are 85 acres of lush parklands...a mile of white sandy beach...one of the finest inland waterway marinas along the entire East Coast. Nearby waters abound with game fish and water fowl. Fresh salt air breezes contribute to a feeling of utter relaxation.

"...You'll want to enjoy the warm friendly atmosphere of our Dockside Hearth lounge and restaurant. As the sun sets over the water, savor your favorite cocktail while the chef prepares a superlative dinner.

"Windmill Point is as easily accessible as it is wonderfully secluded. The resort is less than 3 hours from Washington, D.C., only 1½ hours from Richmond, and less than an hour from both Williamsburg and Jamestown."

THE TIDES INN
Irvington, Virginia
804 / 438-5000

Business Season: March 19 to January 3

Hours: lunch—1 PM to 2 PM, dinner—7 PM to 9 PM, Sunday seafood buffet—1 PM to 9 PM

Waterview: Carter's Creek / Rappahannock River

Credit Cards: MasterCard, Visa, American Express

House Specialties: soft shell crabs, crab cakes, imperial crab, sauteed Chesapeake trout filets, scallops Newburg, oyster cocktail, oysters on the half shell

According to the menu...
"Captain John Smith may have said it best. 'Within is a country that may have the prerogative over the most pleasant places known, for large and pleasant navigable rivers, heaven and earth never agreed better to frame a place for man's habitation.'
"Part of this area is Irvington, a small town settled by John Carter in 1649. Rich in history, Irvington was home to most of the first families of Virginia. Its descendants read like 'who's who' in history books."
Be sure to stop at the Tides Inn. The menu will vary depending on when you arrive. Here is what I was offered: native herring in sour cream, chilled beef rolls Wellington, Louisiana shrimp Arnaud—and these were just the appetizers. Soups included iced fresh melon, cheddar cheese, and country ham; salads listed were bibb lettuce with vinaigrette dressing, or grapefruit sections and avocado pear slices. Main courses included medallion of fresh pork, 6-ounce filet mignon, and baked Chesapeake Bay trout topped with oyster sauce. Selected vegetables were served with honey bran muffins and Sally Lund bread.
As you can see, the Tides Inn is for the discriminating diner. You'll have your choice from seven main courses, or check out one of the seasonal buffets by the pool. And don't forget to try the desserts.

THE TIDES LODGE
One St. Andrews Lane
Irvington, Virginia
804 / 438-6000

Business Season: mid-March to December

Hours: open daily—lunch 12 noon to 2 PM, late lunch 4 PM to 6 PM, dinner 7 PM to 9 PM

Waterview: Carter's Creek / Rappahannock River

Credit Cards: Visa and MasterCard

House Specialties: clams on the half shell, oysters on the half shell, crab cakes, imperial crab, native fish filet, seafood chowder

All around the Chesapeake Bay, you will find many historic towns and villages. Each offers the seafood lover a different atmosphere, but definitely check out Irvington. While you're there, be sure to dine at the Tides Lodge. Here's what the menu has to say.

"The sun has set, but your day isn't over. After cocktails overlooking our marina, [have] a highly praised dinner in the Royal Stewart Dining Room— well known for its innovative cuisine. Or, dine on seafood delicacies at the panoramic informal Binnacle. After dinner, perhaps [you'd like] a moonlight cruise on one of our private yachts, or dancing and an after dinner drink. For those who haven't quite had their fill, we have lighted tennis and putting. [Or, go back] to your room where the maid has left a mint on your pillow and relax with a cable TV movie or enjoy your own private balcony. The end of a perfect day, and then tomorrow. . ."

THE UPPER DECK RESTAURANT
Route 624
Mollusk, Virginia
804 / 462-7400

Business Season: March through November—Friday and Saturday only, Memorial Day through Labor Day—Thursday through Saturday

Hours: open daily—4:30 PM to 9 PM

Waterview: Greenvale Creek / Rappahannock River

Credit Cards: none

House Specialties: seafood buffet

Milton and Gayle Conrad opened the Upper Deck Restaurant in April 1986 on top of the Old Oyster House. The downstairs, under the name of E.J. Conrad and Sons Seafood, is a seafood market that offers all types of seafood. Upstairs, where Milton took over from his dad who was a waterman, is a small pine-paneled restaurant with many ceiling fans.

The Upper Deck offers no menu but features a seafood buffet and daily specials. A blackboard posted outside lists the day's special items. My lucky catch was fried oysters, spiced shrimp, crab balls, broiled fish, crab legs, salad bar, potato salad, cole slaw, shrimp salad, fruit salad, and clam chowder.

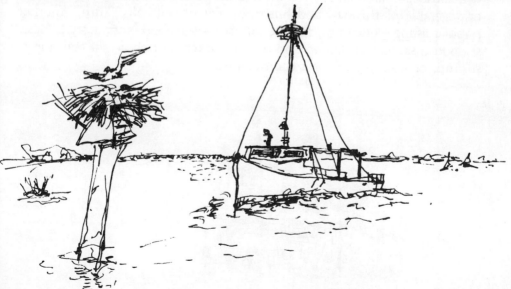

HORN HARBOR HOUSE
Route 810
Burgess, Virginia
804 / 453-3351

Business Season: April through November

Hours: Monday, Wednesday, and Thursday—5 PM to 9 PM; Friday and Saturday—5 PM to 10 PM; Sunday—4 PM to 9 PM; Tuesday—closed

Waterview: Great Wicomico River

Credit Cards: none

House Specialties: backfin crab cakes, fried seafood platter, broiled seafood platter, stuffed shrimp, crab cakes, filet of flounder, fried soft shell crabs, imperial crab

Once you have reached Burgess, turn off Route 200 onto 699 and follow it to Route 663. Then take Route 810, or just follow the signs to Harbor House. A large inviting front porch with six long benches makes for easy sitting. Pine trees abound, and there are many high bluffs. The view of the narrow river is enhanced by the many boats on the water. Harbor House even has a steamboat of its own. It's on the menu. The selection includes steamed lobster tail, crab, clams, shrimp, and crab legs, all deliciously prepared and served with baked potato or french fries, cole slaw or vegetable of the day, and hush puppies or hot rolls. Yum. Another popular listing—one of my favorites, in fact—is seafood Norfolk style. Here, seafood is sauteed in lemon and butter. Order your choice of crab meat, shrimp, or scallops, or try a combination.

ARBUCKLES
1101 Sophia Street
Fredericksburg, Virginia
703 / 371-0775

Business Season: all year

Hours: Monday through Thursday—11:30 AM to 10 PM, Friday and Saturday—11:30 AM to 11 PM, Sunday brunch—11 AM to 2 PM, dinner to 10 PM

Waterview: Rappahannock River

Credit Cards: MasterCard, Visa, American Express, Diners Card

House Specialties: clam chowder, broiled stuffed mushrooms, shrimp cocktail, crab meat cocktail, stuffed bay scallops, crab imperial, stuffed shrimp, broiled or fried shrimp, crab cakes, broiled mariner's platter, crab Norfolk, crab puffs

Arbuckles is located in the historic district of downtown Fredericksburg. My winter visit recalls the snow that blanketed the sloping river bank, and I remember how nice it was being seated by the fireplace that set the scene for the delightful meal served us.

The mighty Rappahannock River flows from the Blue Ridge mountains 165 miles—three-fourths the length of Virginia—before emptying into the Bay. In the spring, this is the site of the Rappahannock White Water Race, but this winter the water was still with not a ripple. Plenty of trees in the snow offered a pleasant calming effect. I was inside where I wanted to be, sitting by the window beside a nice warm fire and eating good food.

I was greeted by one of the owners, Charles Weimer, who told me the building had its own ghost story. It had once housed a cola plant, a car wash, an antique store, and was a warehouse when the present owners took over. The old wood was salvaged and used throughout the decor. In fact, during the renovation, they found an old coffee crate with the name "Arbuckles" on it—hence the restaurant's name.

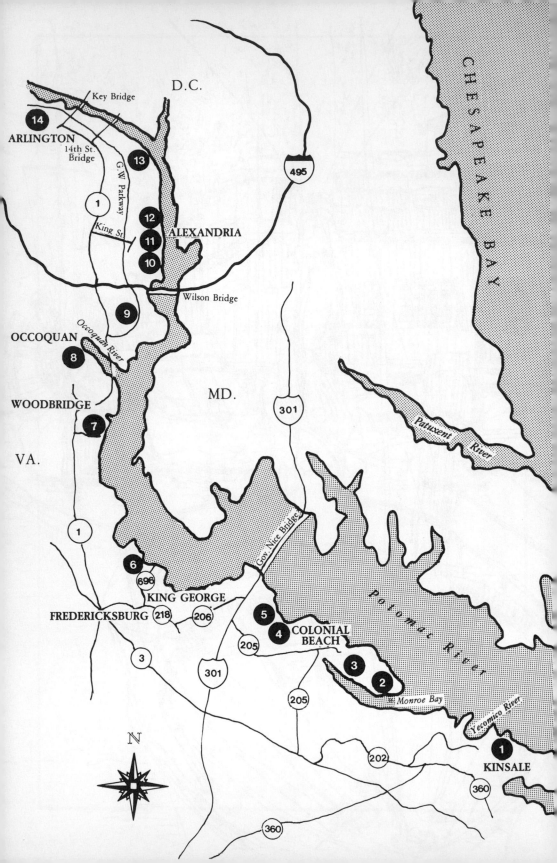

Potomac River
Virginia Shoreline
Waterfront Dining

INCLUDES: *Kinsale, Colonial Beach, King George, Woodbridge, Occoquan, Alexandria, and Arlington, Virginia.*

1. The Mooring Restaurant
2. Parker's Crab Shore
3. Steve's Seafood Restaurant
4. The Happy Clam Seafood Restaurant
5. Wilkerson's Seafood Restaurant
6. Fairview Beach Crab House
7. Pilot House
8. Sea Sea and Company Restaurant
9. Cedar Knoll Inn
10. Dandy Cruise Ship
11. Union Street Public House
12. The Seaport Inn
13. Potowmack Landing
14. The View Restaurant

THE MOORING RESTAURANT
Route 608
Kinsale, Virginia
804 / 472-2971

Business Season: all year

Hours: Friday through Sunday—5 PM to 9 PM

Waterview: Yeocomico River

Credit Cards: Visa and MasterCard

House Specialties: seafood pie, shrimp scampi, imperial crab, crab cocktail, broiled filet of flounder, seafood Newburg, crab cake platter, seafood platter, broiled scallops, stuffed shrimp, soft shell crabs

The town of Kinsale, settled around 1700, was named by settlers for their home in Ireland. Take the time to walk around the old town, breathe in the country air, and gaze at the Yeocomico River used by watermen who take stakes and mark their oyster beds.

The Mooring Restaurant is tucked in a cove on the outskirts of town at the water's edge. The white shingled building with its beautiful lawn and climbing roses is at the end of a mile-long gravel drive in a lovely wooded setting. You enter the restaurant through an enclosed porch filled with long tables and benches that cater to the boating crowd when the marina is full. The inside offers delicious casual dining. Dark paneling, red plaid carpet, a large fireplace, and picture windows overlook the park-like setting.

When we visited on Halloween, we found no tricks, only treats. The staff was well prepared in their ghost and goblin costumes. This little poem was printed on the place mat.

"In this place on the Northern Neck,
At the bar or on the deck,
Divinely you can dine
With cocktails, beer or wine.
Come to the Mooring—it's worth the trek!"

PARKER'S CRAB SHORE

1016 Monroe Bay Avenue
Colonial Beach, Virginia
804 / 224-7090

Business Season: April through October

Hours: open daily—11:30 AM to 9 PM

Waterview: Monroe Bay

Credit Cards: none

House Specialties: crab cakes, imperial crab, crab salad, crab Norfolk, soft crab, steamed shrimp, filet of fish, fried clams, fried oysters, steamed crabs

When you arrive at Colonial Beach, the first thing you should do is drive through the tiny streets of this town on the Potomac River. When you go up Monroe Bay Avenue, you'll pass a sign that reads "Slow— Duck Crossing." So, slowly make your way to Parker's Crab Shore. Watch for its green shingles and cobblestone store front. Inside you'll find a large room filled with green tables and green benches and fans on the ceiling. The day I was there, "Mona Lisa" was playing on the old juke box in the center of the room, creating an air of nostalgia.

Owners John Fenwick and Robert Jenkins take pride in their place and it shows. Their seafood dinner includes fried shrimp, crab cake, fried scallops, filet of fish, and shoestring clams served with french fries and cole slaw. If you want soft shell crab as well, it's two dollars extra. My order was quickly filled.

It's time you visited Parker's and the nearby attractions like Stratford Hall Plantation and George Washington's birthplace.

STEVE'S SEAFOOD RESTAURANT

11 Monroe Bay Avenue
Colonial Beach, Virginia
804 / 224-7360

Business Season: all year

Hours: open daily—11 AM to 10 PM

Waterview: Monroe Bay

Credit Cards: Visa and MasterCard

House Specialties: fried oysters, crab cakes, soft shell crabs, crab imperial, fried shrimp, shrimp creole, broiled seafood combination platter, Norfolk combination platter, steamed crabs

A small pitcher of ice-cold Pabst beer, a dozen delightfully steamed hard shell crabs, and a table at the water's edge was all I needed to be happy. A ship's steering wheel, lantern style lights, numerous ceiling fans, and 11 tables created an inviting setting. The larger rear room held the bar and additional tables.

Whatever draws you to Colonial Beach, whether it's the annual Fourth of July celebration with a chicken barbecue, the boardwalk art show and sale, or simply the desire to see an historic location, be sure to give Steve's a try.

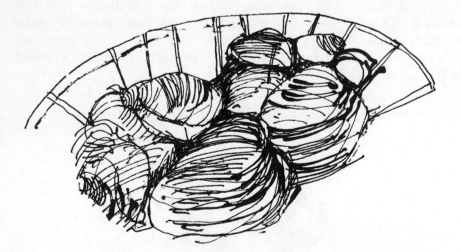

THE HAPPY CLAM SEAFOOD RESTAURANT

Route 205, Colonial Beach Avenue
Colonial Beach, Virginia
804 / 224-0248

Business Season: all year

Hours: open daily—11:30 AM to 9 PM

Waterview: Potomac River

Credit Cards: Visa and MasterCard

House Specialties: fried clams, fried oysters, crab cakes, broiled seafood kabobs, deviled crabs, broiled fish, stuffed flounder, steamed shrimp, soft shell crabs, shrimp Norfolk, crab Norfolk

"The Happy Clam is located on the former terminus of the Morgantown, MD—Potomac Beach car ferry. The pilings jutting out into the Potomac from the shore at the Happy Clam were formerly the pier onto which the ferry docked. The car ferry was the quickest way to get from Maryland to the Northern Neck of Virginia before the Potomac River bridge was built in 1941. The bridge can be seen from the restaurant on clear days. Since the construction of the bridge, the car ferry has stopped its hourly trips. And the remains of the pilings have become the nesting site of an osprey family. The osprey is a large bird, closely related to the eagle. Look for their nest; and in the summer months, their young.

"At the Happy Clam, we serve fresh local products whenever possible. The Potomac River provides much of the crab, fish, and oysters we serve. Just off our shoreline, crabpot floats dot the river and oyster boats work the water ways. A local farm winery, Ingleside Plantation, produces one of the wines we offer. Our chowders and desserts are all homemade.

"The Happy Clam is located in Westmoreland County, a vacationland filled with scenic attractions and historic land marks. Surrounded by natural waterways, it has been a popular resort area since colonial times.

WILKERSON'S SEAFOOD RESTAURANT

Route 205
Colonial Beach, Virginia
804 / 224-7117

Business Season: March to mid-November

Hours: open daily—11:30 AM to 9 PM

Waterview: Potomac River

Credit Cards: Visa and MasterCard

House Specialties: stuffed shrimp, fried shrimp, broiled fish dinner, fried oyster platter, crab meat Norfolk, crab meat Newburg, spiced shrimp, combination platters, steamed crabs

Three good reasons for visiting Colonial Beach are the beach, history, and food. A good place for food is Wilkerson's. Here is a sampling from the Wilkerson's menu.

Jumbo Shrimp Stuffed with Crab Meat
French Fried Shrimp
Filet of Fish Dinner (Broiled or Fried)
Crab Cake Platter
Fried Oyster Platter
Deep Sea Scallops
Crab Meat Casserole
   Norfolk Style, Newburg Style
Shrimp Casserole
   Norfolk Style, Newburg Style
Crab Meat and Shrimp Casserole
   Norfolk Style, Newburg Style
Spiced Shrimp Platter
Australian Lobster Tail
No. 1 Combination
   Imperial Crab, Crab Cake, Filet of Fish
No. 2 Combination
   Imperial Crab, Soft Shell Crab, Crab Cake
No. 3 Combination
   Soft Shell Crab, Crab Cake, Filet of Fish

FAIRVIEW BEACH CRAB HOUSE

Route 696
Fredericksburg, Virginia
703 / 775-7500

Business Season: Late March to Late September

Hours: Friday—4 PM to 10 PM, Saturday—12 noon to 10 PM, Sunday—12 noon to 9 PM, Monday through Thursday (May 16 through Labor Day)—4 PM to 9 PM

Waterview: Potomac River

Credit Cards: Visa and MasterCard

House Specialties: crab cakes, stuffed flounder, fried shrimp, fried clams, seafood au gratin, broiled seafood combination platter, steamed crabs, soft shell crabs, spiced shrimp

Officially, the Potomac River is part of Maryland; its waters extend to the Virginia shore. In the days when slot machines and gambling were legal in Maryland, many Virginia establishments were built over Maryland waters with a gangplank leading from the Virginia shore. This is a carryback to the days when Maryland had three times as many slot machines as did Las Vegas, and the gangplank allowed Virginia residents the opportunity to gamble without driving across the river.

If you arrive by water, the management of the Fairview Beach Crab House offers a shuttle service. Just moor your boat out in the river and give a short blast of your horn. They will pick you and your party up and after a pleasant meal will return you to your boat.

The restaurant is built on piers and is surrounded by water. The 50-year-old building shows its age. It seems that every winter when the river freezes the building suffers a little damage. Once it was practically destroyed by a hurricane.

"From the bottom of the Bay to the top of the table" came the deliciously savory steamed blue crabs, our first of the season. Owners Ray Stoner, Art Chiavaroli, and Malone Schooler do the crab cooking and use just the correct amount of spice and vinegar. Our group shared the "pavilion platter." It was beautifully prepared and consisted of shrimp, oysters, soft shell crab, crab cake, and ample portions of fresh sea trout. The platter came with hush puppies, crisp french fries, and cole slaw.

If all this is not enough, the restaurant also has its own beach. There is plenty to see and do. We can't wait to return.

PILOT HOUSE
16216 Neabsco Road
Woodbridge, Virginia
703 / 221-1010

Business Season: all year

Hours: Tuesday through Sunday—5 PM to 11 PM

Waterview: Neabsco Creek / Potomac River

Credit Cards: American Express, Diners Club, Visa, MasterCard

House Specialties: clams on the half shell, oysters Rockefeller, cold seafood combination platter, stuffed shrimp, flounder stuffed with imperial crab, soft shell crab, crab cakes, broiled perch

Once a barge and now built to look like a paddle boat, the Pilot House is the most nautical in decor of any restaurant I visited. You can't look anywhere without seeing a stuffed fish, lobster traps, crab traps, nets on the windows, oars on the walls. Even the waitresses are dressed in red, white, and blue sailor suits. Open since 1970, the restaurant is owned by Donald Hill. The menu offers 30 seafood and 7 meat entrees. Whatever your selection, you can be assured of a wonderful meal.

The large windows look out to a marina, and across the Neabsco Creek is a state park where eagles have been sighted. The creek was named for an Indian village, which translated means "at the point of rock." Ocean-going vessels used this creek until about 1840 for trade in ship building, grain, lumber, railroad ties, and barrels.

SEA SEA AND COMPANY RESTAURANT

201 Mill Street
Occoquan, Virginia
703 / 494-1365

Business Season: all year

Hours: Monday through Friday—11 AM to 11:30 PM, Saturday and Sunday—12 noon to 11 PM

Waterview: Occoquan River

Credit Cards: MasterCard, Visa, American Express, Carte Blanche, Diners Club, Choice

House Specialties: shrimp and scallop combination, swordfish steak, fried oysters, catch of the day, mariner's platter, crab soup, clam chowder, clams casino, crab puffs, crab imperial, shrimp scampi

The upper Potomac River abounds in historic towns. Among the most interesting, and perhaps least explored, places is Occoquan. Occoquan means, in the Doque Indian language, "at the end of the water."

The Sea Sea and Company Restaurant offers two levels overlooking the treelined banks of the river. The day I was there, the water was teaming with life. Small boats plyed the river, and kids splashed and floated in large black inner tubes. I sat in a large L-shaped dining room with nice windows and high ceilings. Healthy looking plants added to the decor. The menu had this poem written on it:

> "A little of that, a little of this,
> A menu selection you won't want to miss.
> Whatever your preference this evening for dinner,
> An Occoquan favorite would sure be a winner."

CEDAR KNOLL INN
Mount Vernon Parkway
Alexandria, Virginia
703 / 360-7880

Business Season: all year

Hours: open daily—11:30 AM to 10 PM

Waterview: Potomac River

Credit Cards: Visa, MasterCard, Diners Club

House Specialties: Norfolk combination seafood platter, clams on the half shell, oysters on the half shell, surf 'n' turf

The menu tells you this interesting story.

Cedar Knoll was named for the tall cedar trees that surround the building and the lovely knoll that it nests on overlooking the Potomac River. It is just a stone's throw from historic Mount Vernon and, in fact, was once owned by George Washington, who purchased it on June 20, 1752. Although the Inn has been through several significant changes over time, it still retains much of its original charm.

The former farmhouse that is the Cedar Knoll Inn today was constructed in the late 1800's as a tenant dwelling for the 115.34 acre plantation called "Marsland on the Potomac." The property included the stately main house (now known as the "Tower House" adjoining Cedar Knoll on the south side), a two story boathouse, and a barn. "In 1909, Dr. Bliss [the owner] was playing cards upstairs in the boathouse and lost the property in a poker game. He then moved across the river to Maryland and built a new home that is a close replica of the Tower House...During World War I the Tower House was used as a convalescent hospital for troops returning from the front."

Cedar Knoll today is open 7 days a week for lunch and dinner and offers a brunch on Sundays. There is music for dancing on Friday and Saturday evenings, and a fashion show every Tuesday at lunch. The Inn invites you to enjoy a good meal in beautiful surroundings."

DANDY CRUISE SHIP
Prince Street
Alexandria, Virginia
703 / 683-6076

Business Season: all year

Hours: lunch (2½ hours)—boarding time 11:30 AM, dinner (3 hours)—boarding time 6:30 PM

Waterview: Potomac River

Credit Cards: Visa, MasterCard, Carte Blanche, Choice, American Express, Diners Club

House Specialties: stuffed shrimp, filet of flounder, poached salmon

Are you looking for a unique dining experience? If so, cross the gangplank and board the Dandy, a cruise ship that plys the upper Potomac River. Proprietors of the Dandy are Nina Wilson and Al Futress. Leaving from its dock in historic Old Town Alexandria, the Dandy will take you on a lunch or dinner cruise up the Potomac River to the Kennedy Center. Enjoy spectacular views of the nation's monuments. The Dandy's accommodations offer pleasant dining afloat in the tradition of the restaurant riverboats that ply the Seine through the heart of Paris.

During the dinner cruise, guests enjoy a delicious four-course meal accompanied by easy listening music. There is dancing to a variety of musical styles. The waterfront and picturesque yacht harbor makes this cruise ideal for the newcomer as well as an economic way to entertain family or out-of-town guests.

UNION STREET PUBLIC HOUSE

121 South Union Street
Alexandria, Virginia
703 / 548-1785

Business Season: all year

Hours: Monday through Saturday—11:30 AM to 1:30 AM, Sunday—11 AM to 1:30 AM

Waterview: Potomac River

Credit Cards: American Express, Visa, MasterCard

House Specialties: lobster fritters, oysters on the half shell, clams on the half shell, cream of crab soup, lobster Norfolk, crab cakes, lobster salad, crab meat salad, lobster, scallops, swordfish chowder, oyster and turkey pot pie, smoked fish

This pub and oyster bar is a fun place to be. The building, on the west side of Union Street, is about a block and a half from the water. Inside, the aged brick walls and dark wood are enhanced by many little corners and cozy nooks. At the oyster bar, the tiny floor tiles and neon lights of old beer companies create nostalgia. But the upstairs dining room is where you will enjoy the best view. Look through the large windows across the shimmering waters of the Potomac River, and you may see Alexandria's own tall ship, the Alexandria Schooner. Here's some information about this popular tall ship.

"With her distinctive red sails, the 125-foot long schooner is a classic Scandinavian vessel built in Sweden in 1929 and then remodelled for passengers in the 1970's. In 1976 Alexandria placed third in the Trans Atlantic Tall Ships Race from England to New York and took second place in the 1980 Tall Ships Race. She also participated in OpSail '76 in New York Harbor, as well as the 1986 celebrations to re-dedicate the Statue of Liberty.''

THE SEAPORT INN

6 King Street
Alexandria, Virginia
703 / 549-2341

Business Season: all year

Hours: open daily—11 AM to 10 PM

Waterview: Potomac River

Credit Cards: Visa, MasterCard, Diners Card, American Express

House Specialties: oysters on the half shell, crab meat cocktail, stuffed clams, turtle soup, oyster stew, clam chowder, fried oysters, crab cakes, soft shell crab, stuffed shrimp, catch of the day, seafood platter

The menu tells the following story.

"The Seaport Inn was erected prior to 1765 by John Patterson who built some of the earliest houses in Alexandria as well as making repairs at Mount Vernon for General Washington.

"Patterson built well. The walls of the Seaport Inn of stone and oyster shell mortar are twenty-eight inches thick. On the Great Bearing Beam, fourteen inches wide by eighteen deep and twenty-five feet long, may be found the mark of the adz wielded by Patterson's workmen over two-hundred years ago. Colonel John Fitzgerald, General Washington's military Aide-de-Camp, purchased the building in 1778. The top floor of the structure housed a sail loft. Here, squatted men [were] busy with needle and cord, sewing and lacing the great pieces of canvas into sails. In the early days of the Seaport Inn, Alexandria was the second largest seaport in colonial America. [The first was Boston.]

"President Washington and his friend, Colonel Fitzgerald, spent many pleasant days and nights here recalling their military experiences and toasting their business enterprises. We invite you to do the same within these historic walls."

167

POTOWMACK LANDING
Daingerfield Island
George Washington Memorial Parkway
Alexandria, Virginia
703 / 548-0001

Business Season: all year

Hours: open daily—lunch 11 AM to 2:30 PM, dinner 5:30 PM to 10 PM

Waterview: Potomac River

Credit Cards: American Express, Visa, MasterCard, Diners Club

House Specialties: cioppino, crab cakes, crab Benedict, crab file gumbo, oysters on the half shell, catch of the day

The menu tells the story.

"Potowmack Landing lies within a short cruise of four major rivers, the fertile Chesapeake Bay, and the great Atlantic Ocean. So we are able to offer you an extensive selection of the very freshest seafood every day.

"To enhance the flavor of our broiled seafood selections, we cook with mesquite wood. This pleasantly aromatic wood from the deserts of the Americas burns hotter and more evenly than charcoal, sealing in the delicate, natural juices of seafood, beef and vegetables.

"16 June, 1608—

'...The River of Potowmack. Fish lying so thicke with their heads above water. For want of nets (our barge driving amongst them) we attempted to catch them with a frying pan: But we found it to be a bad instrument to catch fish with. Neither better fish, nor more plenty, had any of us ever seen in any place so swimming in water.'

"Almost 380 years have passed since Captain John Smith entered that observation in his log as he sailed past this island. The mighty Potomac still courses almost 400 miles from tiny streams in Garrett County down over Great Falls, past Potowmack Landing, and out into the Chesapeake Bay. The Piscataway, Susquehanna, and Seneca Indians are gone now, and a great city has grown on the shores and in the once wild forests. But the mighty river whose name means, 'they are coming by water' and 'river of swans' remains."

THE VIEW RESTAURANT
1401 Lee Highway
Arlington, Virginia
703 / 524-6400

Business Season: all year

Hours: open daily—6 PM to 10 PM, Sunday brunch—10 AM to 2 PM

Waterview: Potomac River

Credit Cards: American Express, Diners Card, MasterCard, Visa

House Specialties: shrimp cocktail, oysters on the half shell, baked lump crab meat, lobster bisque, swordfish, sole, sea scallops, poached salmon

There's something special about the view atop the Marriott Hotel's 14 stories where one looks out at the Washington shoreline with all its memorials. It's spectacular and one not to be missed. But be warned—this is a glamorous restaurant with more tuxedos than an Italian wedding. The menu is short and the prices high, but the view's worth the visit. The service is impeccable. The restaurant is near Key Bridge in Rosslyn, a business district of Arlington.

The menu lists several appetizers. Among my favorites are prime oysters on the half shell and jumbo gulf shrimp cocktail. You may choose from a selection of sumptuous seafood featuring baked lump crab meat imperial style, or beluga caviar, each served with chilled imported vodka.

Entrees include grilled swordfish, steak, poached Atlantic salmon, sole, broiled lobster tail, gulf shrimp, sea scallops, and the ever popular surf and turf. The restaurant asks that you let the chef know if you have a request in regard to your food preparation or are on any special diet. But don't look at the prices—just the view.

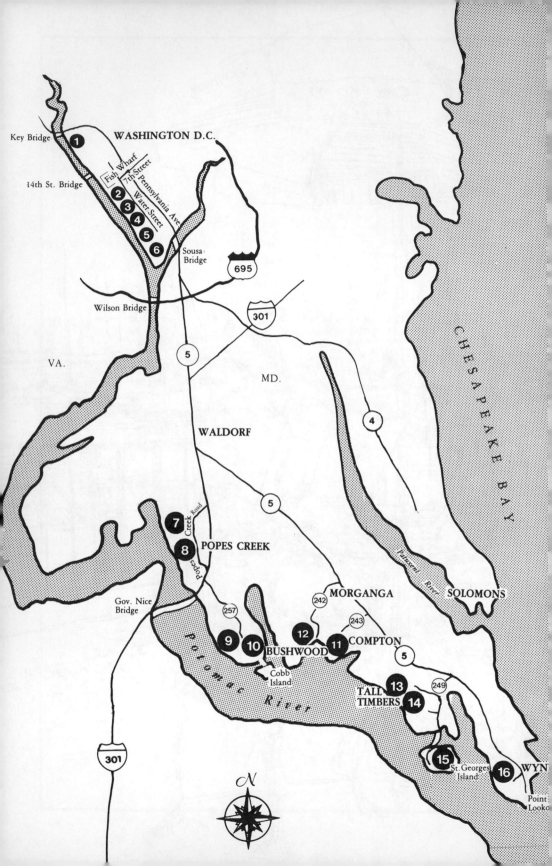

Potomac River
Washington D.C., Maryland Shoreline
Waterfront Dining

INCLUDES: *Northwest and Southwest, Washington, D.C.; Popes Creek, Cobb Island, Bushwood, Compton, Tall Timbers, Valley Lee, St. George's Island, and Wynne, Maryland.*

1. Tony and Joe's Seafood Place
2. Le Rivage
3. Phillips Flagship
4. Hogate's Seafood Restaurant
5. Pier 7 Restaurant
6. The Gangplank
7. Robertson's Crab House
8. Captain Billy's Crab House
9. Captain John's Seafood Restaurant
10. Shymansky's Restaurant
11. Dock 'O' the Bay
12. The Captain's Table
13. The Reluctant Navigator
14. Cedar Cove Inn
15. Evan's Seafood Restaurant
16. Scheible's Restaurant

TONY AND JOE'S SEAFOOD PLACE
3000 K Street, N.W.
Washington, D.C.
202 / 944-4545

Business Season: all year

Hours: open daily—11 AM to 11 PM

Waterview: Potomac River

Credit Cards: Visa, MasterCard, American Express, Diners Card

House Specialties: oysters on the half shell, clams on the half shell, clam chowder, steamed crabs, crab soup, crab cakes, broiled blue fish, crab imperial, crab au gratin, stuffed shrimp, seafood platter, fried oysters, fish of the day

Take a stroll in Georgetown where square-rigged sailing ships and schooners used to wait in the Potomac River for loads of Maryland tobacco, and where carriages used to clatter down cobblestone streets. Georgetown started out as a bustling colonial seaport, but evolved into a swank part of Washington, D.C. Today Georgetown is a place to abandon your car and walk around. It is crowded with people, shops, restaurants, historic sites, and even some quiet places where you can escape all the confusion.

If you want great seafood, a great place to get it is at Tony and Joe's, serving "the freshest seafood at the best prices possible." The menu changes daily. From your seat you will see Washington's most spectacular Potomac River view, including Watergate, the Key Bridge, and Roosevelt Island, just to mention a few.

LE RIVAGE
1000 Water Street, S.W.
Washington, D.C.
202 / 488-8111

Business Season: all year

Hours: Monday through Friday—lunch 11:30 AM to 2:30 PM, dinner 5 PM to 9 PM

Waterview: Washington Channel / Potomac River

Credit Cards: MasterCard, Visa, American Express, Diners Club

House Specialties: soft shell crabs, crab Norfolk, crab cakes, crab imperial, fish of the day, broiled scallops, stuffed flounder, stuffed shrimp

Situated high above the trees overlooking the municipal fish wharf, the harbor, and East Potomac Park, this French restaurant offers perhaps the best view of the southwest Washington waterfront.

Our luncheon visit found it filled and noisy, so we selected the outdoor deck. It was a windy day, but the deck tables were shielded by large beach umbrellas stamped "Campari."

I ordered the soft shell crabs. They arrived hot and were seasoned with fine herbs accompanied by plenty of fresh rolls with whipped butter. An ice cold Kronenbourg beer topped the meal.

175

PHILLIPS FLAGSHIP

900 Water Street, S.W.
Washington, D.C.
202 / 488-8515

Business Season: all year

Hours: open daily—11 AM to 11 PM, closed Christmas

Waterview: Washington Channel / Potomac River

Credit Cards: MasterCard, Visa, Choice, American Express, Diners Club

House Specialties: clams on the half shell, oysters on the half shell, crab claw cocktail, steamer buckets, crab soup, crab cakes, fresh fish of the day, fried seafood platter, steamed seafood platter, crab imperial, fried oysters, steamed scallops

Brice Phillips did not start out to be a restauranteur. He was working in the crab packing business when he began selling crabs in a tar paper shack. The business has grown since then to become "Maryland's Largest," listed in the top 100 restaurants in the country. Enjoy this casual, relaxed atmosphere in his newest location at the Washington waterfront.

My most recent visit recalls "DW's" peach wine cooler—a refreshing blend of crisp wine, freshly squeezed citrus juices, and just the right punch of peach to satisfy the best of summer thirsts. The featured appetizer was steamed spiced shrimp—a half pound of shrimp served with spicy cocktail sauce. The featured entree was cioppino—a classic Italian seafood stew full of half a lobster tail, mussels, scallops, clams, and oysters simmered in basic marinara sauce, served with garlic bread.

Another featured selection is the Summer Seafood Feast. And a feast it is. It includes a cup of vegetable soup, six mussels, one snow crab, four large blue crabs, half a pound of steamed shrimp, corn on the cob, sliced tomatoes, and for dessert, mouthwatering watermelon.

HOGATES SEAFOOD RESTAURANT

800 Water Street
Washington, D.C.
800 / 424-9169, X25

Business Season: all year

Hours: weekdays—11 AM to 11 PM, Friday and Saturday—11 AM to midnight, Sunday—10:30 AM to 10 PM

Waterview: Washington Channel / Potomac River

Credit Cards: Discover, MasterCard, Visa, Choice, Diners Club, Carte Blanche

House Specialties: steamed mussels, fried oysters, steamed clams, oysters on the half shell, crab meat cocktail, clam chowder, snapping turtle soup, shrimp salad, 'Hogate's Original' 1938 mariner's platter, crab imperial, crab cakes, catch of the day

This is the Hogate's story.

"Hogate's Spectacular Seafood Restaurant has been a Washington tradition for over forty years. We like to think of it as the other Washington Monument. It originally began as a small seafood stand in Ocean City, New Jersey in 1928. In 1938, the owners of Hogate's decided to move to Washington, D.C. For 35 years it enjoyed great success and became the place to go in Washington for great seafood. Then, in 1972 the Washington Waterfront area underwent a complete redevelopment program. At this time, Hogate's moved from across the street on Maine Avenue to its present location overlooking the Potomac River. Originally named after a family physician, John Hogate Whittaker, Hogate's has become one of the largest and best known seafood restaurants in the United States.

"Our reputation for quality and value has grown over the years. House specialties like the 'Original Mariner's Platter', "Snapper Soup' and 'Hot Rum Buns' have generated their own loyal following. Every day our chefs bake our own fresh rum buns, make our own soups and prepare our own seafood specialties to your order.

"These traditions that have helped us establish our reputation for great seafood dining are still with us almost a half century later. Hogate's has become a tradition only through the fine reputation our guests have given us. That is why Hogate's has become Washington's freshest tradition."

PIER 7 RESTAURANT
650 Water Street, S.W.
Washington, D.C.
202 / 554-2500

Business Season: all year

Hours: Monday through Friday—11:15 AM to 11:15 PM, Saturday—4 PM to 11:15 PM, Sunday—2 PM to 10 PM

Waterview: Washington Channel / Potomac River

Credit Cards: MasterCard, Visa, Diners Club

House Specialties: oysters on the half shell, crab gumbo, Boston clam chowder (Friday only), stuffed flounder, seafood Newburg, stuffed baked shrimp, crab imperial, crab cakes, cold seafood combination platter, bouillabaisse

Part of the Channel Inn Hotel, Pier 7 is located on the waterfront off Maine Avenue and 7th Street. If you're fortunate enough to time your visit right, as we did outs, you may see the President's yacht docked at the end of the pier. Inside, the decor is like the inside of a ship at sea. The deep mahogony walls are decorated with ship's gauges, gears, and pressure valves, and pictures of various sailing vessels hang in gold frames with red mats. There are red tablecloths and red and blue carpeting throughout. The red and blue theme is continued in the employees' dress.

Your first visit to the Pier 7 Restaurant will lead to many more. My first visit recalls large, mildly spicy crab cakes with a pleasant aftertaste. The cole slaw was rich and creamy, the oven fries crisp and hot. For great seafood eating, I suggest the catch of the day. Or choose from 16 fresh fish entrees such as filet of sole almondine, broiled salmon steak, and Florida red snapper.

THE GANGPLANK
600 Water Street, S.W.
Washington, D.C.
202 / 554-5000

Business Season: all year

Hours: weekdays—lunch 11:30 AM to 2 PM; weekends—lunch 11:30 AM to 3 PM, dinner 5:30 PM to 10 PM

Waterview: Washington Channel / Potomac River

Credit Cards: Visa, American Express, MasterCard

House Specialties: clams on the half shell, clams casino, oysters Rockefeller, steak and stuffed shrimp, seafood au gratin, fresh catch of the day, crab cakes, stuffed shrimp, seafood Norfolk, broiled combination platter

The menu tells about the interesting history of the waterfront:
"The Gangplank Restaurant floats in some very historic waters. A century ago the present waterfront area was a vital commercial and transportation lifeline to the Nation's Capital, and the port was teeming with hundreds of boats of all kinds.

"Two, three, and four masted schooners unloaded cargoes as diverse as granite blocks and ice from Maine, timber from North Carolina, paving stones from Belgium, lime, coal, seafood, produce, and dozens of other commodities. Similarly, passenger steamers left regularly for Norfolk, Baltimore and other more distant ports.

"The Washington waterfront is again a hub of commercial and recreational activity; the Potomac sparkles again; and two and three masted 'Tall Ships' again mingle with the hundreds of sailing yachts and power cruisers which call the port of Washington home.

"During the late 1950's and the '60's, urban renewal began to change the face of Southwest Washington and, with it, the waterfront—spurred by the commitment of succeeding Presidents to clean up the once proud Potomac. Among the earliest private enterprises to state a belief in the waterfront's future was the Gangplank.

"The Gangplank is proud to have been a part of this dramatic revitalization—and we are pleased to have you as our guests to enjoy the ambience of the harbor. Dine, relax, enjoy the view. In short, 'Welcome Aboard.' "

ROBERTSON'S CRAB HOUSE
Popes Creek Road
Popes Creek, Maryland
301 / 934-9236

Business Season: Memorial Day through Labor Day, closed January and February, open weekends only in March and April

Hours: open daily—11 AM to 9 PM

Waterview: Potomac River

Credit Cards: none

House Specialties: steamed crabs, broiled seafood platter, fish of the day platter, oyster platter, spiced shrimp platter, crab imperial platter

Many people travel to Robertson's just for the Maryland steamed crabs seasoned and cooked in the home-style method famous for more than 50 years. However, if you're a seafood enthusiast, the broiled seafood platter is what you've been searching for. Listen to this listing: jumbo shrimp stuffed with crab meat, petite lobster tail, fish of the day, cherrystone clams, and Bay scallops. Or try the admiral's seafood platter, with its crab cake, deep-fried shrimp, oysters, scallops, and fish of the day. Another good choice is the fish of the day fried to a delicious golden brown, or broiled in a sauce of lemon, parsley, and butter. And if you want, it can be stuffed with crab.

Popes Creek is located 6 miles south of LaPlata, just 3 miles off Route 301, overlooking the Potomac River.

CAPTAIN BILLY'S CRAB HOUSE

Popes Creek Road
Popes Creek, Maryland
301 / 932-4323

Business Season: March to December

Hours: open daily—11 AM to 11 PM

Waterview: Potomac River

Credit Cards: Visa and MasterCard

House Specialties: steamed crabs, seafood platter, fried fantail
shrimp, fried oysters, soft shell crabs, crab cakes

The unique geography and topography of this location made it
especially attractive for various reasons to many people centuries before Europeans first saw it. It was a well-known favorite Indian "feasting ground."
Remains of great mounds of oyster shells have been found on the bluffs
overlooking the Popes Creek outlet to the Potomac River.

The tradition of having a restaurant here on the shores of the Potomac
all started with a modest undertaking around 1930 when Captain Paul
Drinks opened a small eating place that specialized in fresh oysters and
crab. As a boy of nine, Billy Robertson would row his small boat in these
same waters and sell the day's catch to his Uncle Paul. Eventually the
restaurant was sold to someone else. Sixty years later, when the restaurant
became available, Billy decided to bring the modest eating place back under
his family's rule.

Today, Captain Billy welcomes you to try his seafood platter, which
he says is nearly large enough for two. It includes crab cake, fried shrimp,
oysters, catch of the day, and, if the season is right, soft shell crab. Or
try the steamed crabs fresh from the pot. Platters are served with a choice
of french fries, potato salad, or cole slaw, and come with rolls and lemon
wedges. Captain Billy offers three drinks from the bar—"Blue Crab" (spiced
rum and citrus), "Backfin" (fruit juices and rum) and "Buster Crab" (rum,
gin, and pineapple).

CAPTAIN JOHN'S SEAFOOD RESTAURANT

Route 254
Cobb Island, Maryland
301 / 259-2315

Business Season: all year

Hours: open daily—7:30 AM to 11 PM

Waterview: Neal Sound / Potomac River

Credit Cards: MasterCard and Visa

House Specialties: seafood platter, fried oysters, crab cakes, soft shell crabs, stuffed shrimp, imperial crab, steamed crabs, crab soup, oyster stew

"Cobb" is the name given to the male swans located at Neal Sound off the Potomac River. On Cobb Island you may see blue heron waiting patiently for supper on free-standing fish net stakes and osprey building a nest on channel markers. A blustery northwestern wind may force you inside to view the outdoor activity. If you happen to stop at Captain John's, you are in for a treat.

This restaurant is one of the best when it comes to preparing the famous blue crab. Or try Captain John's seafood platter with crab cake, fish, fried shrimp, scallops, fried oysters or soft-shell crab in season, two vegetables, and hot rolls with butter. If you like, you can buy fresh seafood for your return home.

SHYMANSKY'S RESTAURANT
Route 254
Cobb Island, Maryland
301 / 259-2881

Business Season: all year

Hours: open daily—8 AM to midnight

Waterview: Neal Sound / Potomac River

Credit Cards: MasterCard and Visa

House Specialties: crab cakes, crab imperial, cream of crab soup, crab salad, deviled crab, stuffed flounder, soft shell crabs

Blackbeard buried his treasures in numerous spots around the Chesapeake Bay where they were never unearthed. Today the Bay country beckons to the sailor with different treasures—tiny islands of natural beauty, folklore, tradition, history, and fine food.

To many, the powerboat is the way to see the Bay. For others, it's under the sail of a 33' Hunter sailboat. Regardless of your preference, Shymansky's offers you boat rentals, boat slips, a marine store, bar, and restaurant; and if you call ahead, Pat and Butch Shymansky will prepare for your next boat party.

It had been approximately 7 years since my last visit to Shymansky's. I was quick to learn that the room where the pool table once sat had been replaced by a salad bar. The restaurant had been completely renovated and could now seat 250. The marina was so close to my table I could hear the bilge pump chugging endlessly from a small white boat beyond the narrow sound. The view was of tiny beach houses that hugged the shore.

I was made to feel at home, but I was there to try the food, and when my cream of crab soup was served good and hot, I knew that my mission had been accomplished. Next arrived my crab cake. It was a nice size and laden with succulent chunks of backfin crab. I piled it with the excellent fresh homemade tartar sauce.

DOCK 'O' THE BAY

Joehazel Road
Compton, Maryland
301 / 475-3129

Business Season: all year

Hours: Tuesday through Sunday—10 AM to 10 PM

Waterview: Breton Bay / Potomac River

Credit Cards: none

House Specialties: seafood platter, soft shell crabs, steamed oysters, fried oysters, oysters on the half shell, stuffed shrimp, crab cakes, catch of the day, imperial crab

To reach the dining room you must pass through the entrance foyer that provides a view of the open kitchen and friendly bar. The bar ceiling is black, the dining room ceiling white. The 12 tables are brown earth tones. Next to the fireplace is a small aquarium, supported by three cinder blocks and filled with gold and black fish. A stuffed turtle is perched on the floor at the hearth's edge.

The dock platter, crab cakes, imperial crab, stuffed shrimp, and fish of the day are available on a daily basis. Oysters and soft shell crabs are seasonal, but don't let the season stop you. Hurry on down to southern Maryland and sample a tradition.

The area is famous for relaxation, so be sure to allow time for recreation whether it's swimming, tennis, canoeing, or simply walking along the shore.

184

THE CAPTAIN'S TABLE

Route 520, White Neck Road
Bushwood, Maryland
301 / 769-9892

Business Season: all year

Hours: Thursday and Friday—5 PM to 10 PM, Saturday—1 PM to 10 PM, Sunday—brunch 11 AM to 3 PM, dinner to 9 PM

Waterview: Whites Neck Creek / Wicomico River

Credit Cards: none

House Specialties: cream of crab soup, crab soup, oyster stew, oysters on the half shell, oysters casino, broiled scallops, crab cakes, crab imperial, crab meat Norfolk, catch of the day

A late southern Maryland historian once traced this site as far back as the 1600's. In 1880 there was a tavern here known as Bailey's Crab House. More recently, it was known as T's Cove. Today it is The Captain's Table, owned and operated by Bernard and Louise Matthews, who take great pride in it. A plaque on the front door marks it as an historic tavern. In a recent renovation the outside deck was transformed into a lovely screened porch for dining.

The day I dined there, the service was swift. The crab soup was full of fresh vegetables and arrived at the table hot. Broiled stuffed mushrooms, an appetizer, were filled with delicious tidbits of shrimp and crab meat. The captain's platter was a broiled feast of whole lobster, scallops, shrimp, and crab imperial. If the food is always this good, this restaurant will soon be very popular.

To get there, take Route 5 to 242, turn at Morganza, go 8.5 miles, and turn right on 239 and then left on 520. Near the restaurant is the landing site of the Maryland colonists in 1634. The area abounds in open-air markets with fresh local produce, antiques, and curios. The Potomac River Museum stresses the history of the area with archeological exhibits.

THE RELUCTANT NAVIGATOR

Tall Timbers Marina
Tall Timbers, Maryland
301 / 994-1508

Business Season: March to November

Hours: open daily—7 AM to 10 PM

Waterview: Herring Creek / Potomac River

Credit Cards: Visa, MasterCard, Chevron

House Specialties: raw oysters, fried oysters, soft shell crab, crab cake, catch of the day, broiled seafood dinner

Chef Nancy Lee lends her Taiwan Chinese influence and combines it with fresh southern Maryland food. Her delicate blend of herbs and spices highlights the gifts from the sea. Be sure to notice that each menu is a hand-crafted art work. On one side is a picture of a fish or crab, which Nancy does each day. The other side is the menu.

On my visit on the first of May, the daily specials listed fried oysters, shrimp salad, and stuffed sea trout. All meals are served with fresh garden salad, soup, choice of vegetables, hot bread, and tea or coffee. And don't forget to ask about the homemade desserts.

CEDAR COVE INN
Route 249
Valley Lee, Maryland
301 / 994-1418

Business Season: all year

Hours: Monday through Thursday—10 AM to 8 PM; Friday, Saturday, and Sunday—10 AM to 10 PM

Waterview: Herring Creek / Potomac River

Credit Cards: Visa and MasterCard

House Specialties: fried oysters, stuffed flounder, crab cakes, oyster stew, soft shell crabs, shrimp cocktail, shrimp scampi, homemade fish chowder

Turning south on Maryland's Route 5, you make a right turn on Route 249 and look for the large green sign that points the way to a gravel lane. Walk down a tiny walkway through a cove of cedar trees and you will come to a well-kept marina with large boats. The restaurant is located in the basement of a home on the waterfront.

Inside the Cedar Cove Inn are two tiny rooms with room for ten small tables. (The management assured me that they could seat 30.) The bar was made of cinder block. The decor was charming and I was made to feel instantly at home. A green blackboard featured the day's menu— French dip, coveburger, steak and cheese, ham and cheese, chef's salad, fresh tuna salad, and crab cake sandwich. I forked my way through a large crab cake filled with succulent chunks of just-picked crab. The lettuce was crisp and the tomato red and juicy.

At this cosy hideaway, weekend offerings include homemade fish chowder and fried oysters, and a generous portion of plump oysters from Herring Creek. All entrees include crisp garden salad, freshly baked bread, baked potato, fries, broccoli or green beans, and tea or coffee.

EVAN'S SEAFOOD RESTAURANT

Route 249
St. George's Island, Maryland
301 / 994-2299

Business Season: all year

Hours: Tuesday through Friday—4 PM to 11 PM, Saturday and Sunday—12 noon to 11 PM, closed Monday

Waterview: St. George's Creek / St. Mary's River

Credit Cards: none

House Specialties: soft shell crab sandwiches, steamed crabs, crab cakes, crab imperial, seafood platter, fried oyster platter, oyster stew

Captain John Smith called southern Maryland "a delightsome land." You will too once you discover one of life's greatest pleasures—the soft shell crab sandwich!

Soft crabs are blue crabs that have shed their shells. Crabs can best shed their shells in water temperatures over 70 degrees F. In the Chesapeake Bay, soft shell crabs become available in late spring to early fall, with May through August being the best months. Once the water temperatures drop, the molting will slow down.

So time your visit accordingly, and you will find out why this southern Maryland tradition has such a following.

SCHEIBLE'S RESTAURANT

Wynne, Maryland

301 / 872-5185

Business Season: May through October

Hours: open daily—6:30 AM to 10 PM

Waterview: Potomac River

Credit Cards: none

House Specialties: Maryland baked ham, steamed crabs, fresh fish, crab soup, crab cakes, soft shell crabs, oysters—any style, day's catch, broiled shrimp, captain's platter

Home to some of the best fishing in the entire Chesapeake Bay, Point Lookout offers the angler more species of fish, and Scheible's offers more ways to catch them, than any other area of the state. The oldest fishing center in southern Maryland, Scheible's has been serving fishermen for half a century. Outdoor motor boats are for rent, and there is a wonderful picnic area and 500-foot fishing and crabbing dock. Through the restaurant windows you can watch fishing parties returning on the long pier.

Entrees include crab cake, soft shell crabs, the day's catch fried or broiled, and broiled shrimp in garlic butter. The captain's platter includes local fish, clams, shrimp, scallops, soft shell crab, crab cake, and hush puppies. You can order all you can eat of an original recipe called "crabettes," spicy bite-sized crab cakes. This special includes salad bar and french fries, but the management warns, "Please, no sharing."

189

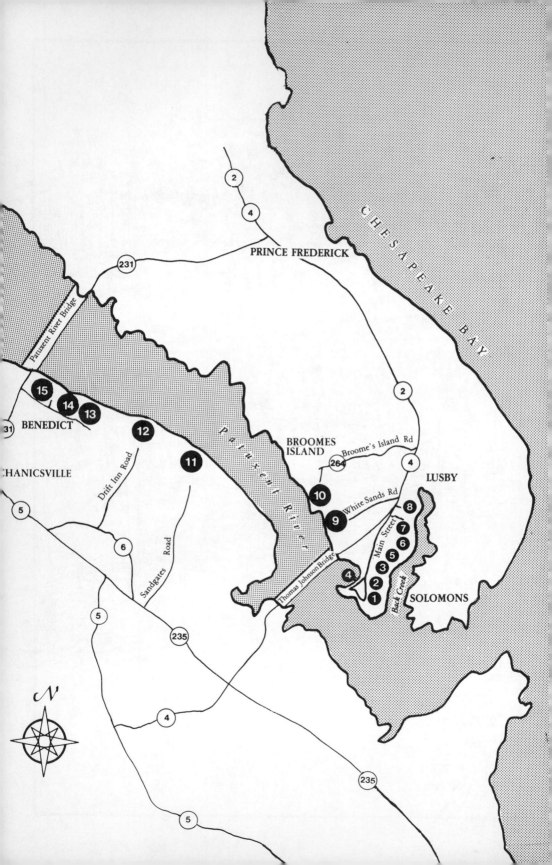

Patuxent River
Waterfront Dining

INCLUDES: Solomons, Lusby, Broomes Island, Mechanicsville, Oraville, and Benedict, Maryland.

1. Harbour View Restaurant
2. Lighthouse Inn
3. Bowen's Inn
4. Solomons Pier Restaurant
5. Dry Dock Restaurant
6. Pier I Restaurant
7. The Naughty Gull
8. The Maryland Way Restaurant
9. Vera's White Sands
10. Gatsby's Dockside Galley
11. Sandgates Inn
12. Drift Inn Seafood
13. Chappelear's Restaurant
14. Shorter's Place
15. Ray's Pier Restaurant

HARBOUR VIEW RESTAURANT

Patuxent Avenue
Solomons, Maryland
301 / 326-3202
301 / 862-3226

Business Season: all year

Hours: open daily—11 AM to 11 PM

Waterview: Back Creek / Patuxent River

Credit Cards: MasterCard, Visa, Choice

House Specialties: catch of the day, oyster platter, fried shrimp platter, crab cake platter, shrimp scampi, mussels scampi, fried oysters, oysters on the half shell, steamed oysters

The following brief history of Solomons is outlined on the menu. "Originally called Bourne's Island (1680), then Somervell's Island (1740), it became known as Solomons Island in 1870 because of Isaac Solomon's oyster packing facilities. His home still stands on the front of the island. In the 19th century, shipyards developed to support the island's fishing fleet. The Marsh Shipyard built schooners and sloops, but became famous for its bugeyes, the forerunner to the skipjack. In the war of 1812, Commodore Joshua Barney's Flotella sailed from here to attack British vessels on the Chesapeake Bay." The deep, protected harbor has been a busy marine center ever since. Come to Solomons, smell the salt air, walk the quaint streets, and when it's time to eat, give the Harbour View a try.

194

LIGHTHOUSE INN
Patuxent Avenue
Solomons, Maryland
301 / 326-2444

Business Season: all year

Hours: open daily—11 AM to 10 PM

Waterview: Back Creek / Patuxent River

Credit Cards: MasterCard and Visa

House Specialties: steamed clams, crab meat cocktail, clams casino, cream of crab soup, catch of the day, fried oysters, shrimp and scallops Norfolk, fried shrimp, crab imperial, crab cakes, soft shell crab, oysters imperial, stuffed flounder, lobster tail

Everyone who arrives in Solomons by car and drives through the tiny town along the sea wall and past the state owned biological pier will soon find the Lighthouse Inn with its natural wood siding and large windows. Inside you can gaze through a two-story wall of glass that looks out over the harbor from the main dining room or the loft-like second floor. The "skipjack bar," the Inn's most unusual feature, was modeled from an actual oyster boat.

The menu features a wide variety of traditional seafood dishes. You "chart your course" through the appetizers, select from "land lubbers' delights," or "set sail" for the catch of the day, stuffed lobster tail, oyster imperial, or the Lighthouse Inn steamed platter. And don't pass up the broiled stuffed flounder.

BOWEN'S INN

Main Street
Solomons, Maryland
301 / 326-2214

Business Season: all year

Hours: open daily—breakfast, lunch, and dinner

Waterview: Back Creek / Patuxent River

Credit Cards: Visa and MasterCard

House Specialties: clams on the half shell, clams casino, crab soup, seafood platter, crab imperial, lobster tail stuffed with crab meat, soft shell crab platter, broiled fish of the day

Bowen's Inn has been serving the needs of Chesapeake watermen since 1918. Calvert County has been called "the charm of the Chesapeake," and nowhere is this more evident than in this waterfront inn. If you want the waterview, then choose the back porch or the outside deck. The main dining area, however, is at the front of the building, away from the water. A blustering wind forced us inside, so we chose the bar, whose turn-of-the-century theme, with its quaint prints, old telephone booth, and old piano, gave us an air of nostalgia.

When we asked the waiter, "What's cookin' now," we were told that the crab soup had just come off the fire and the crab cakes were being freshly made into patties. We selected both and found out why Bowen's Inn, the first restaurant built on Soloman's Island, keeps both visitors and watermen returning for more.

SOLOMONS PIER RESTAURANT
Main Street
Solomons, Maryland
301 / 326-2424

Business Season: all year

Hours: Monday through Saturday—lunch 11:30 AM to 2 PM, dinner 5 PM to 10 PM; Sunday—brunch 10 AM to 2 PM, dinner 5 PM to 10 PM

Waterview: Patuxent River

Credit Cards: American Express, MasterCard, Visa, Choice

House Specialties: seafood platter, stuffed shrimp, steamed seafood dinner, crab fluff, clams on the half shell, clams casino, steamed oysters, steamed seafood platter, seafood stir fry, crab cakes, crab imperial, fried oysters, soft crab platter

The menu tells the story.

"The structure now known as Solomons Pier was originally built in 1919 by Perry (Captain Pert) Evans. Known at that time as the Evans Pavilion, this much smaller version was primarily an ice cream and confectionery parlour.

"In the early 1920's, a waterslide was built to extend from the top of the building so that people could descend in small boats over rollers and splash into the Patuxent River.

"In 1934, the back section was added which later became a movie house. Movies, at that time, cost 15 cents. Because each patron was required to carry his own folding chair into the multi-purpose room, a five cent rebate was given if the chair was returned. In June of 1941, the local newspapers brought excitement to the community with the news of a new and modern movie projector being installed, and movies were shown here until the 1960's.

"Since the 1960's, the building has been a seafood restaurant. In 1984, the structure was rebuilt from the floor upwards and reopened in its present unique style. However, the building still rests on the original pilings driven in 1934! All seating is highlighted by the breathtaking view of the sunset and the spectacular span of the Thomas Johnson Bridge which was built in 1978. The upper levels of the restaurant, the Evans Rooms, display pictures of the building in its different eras."

DRY DOCK RESTAURANT
C Street
Solomons, Maryland
301 / 326-4817

Business Season: all year

Hours: Monday through Thursday—6 PM to 9 PM; Friday and Saturday—5:30 PM to 9:30 PM; Sunday—brunch 10 AM to 2 PM, dinner 5:30 PM to 9 PM; closed Tuesday during off season

Waterview: Back Creek / Patuxent River

Credit Cards: MasterCard, Visa, American Express, Bank America, Choice

House Specialties: shrimp bisque, shrimp scampi, grilled salmon, flounder and crab florentine, scallops, spiced shrimp, crab cakes, soft shell crabs

Once truly an island, Solomons is now joined to the rest of Calvert County, Maryland by a bed of oyster shells, recalling the island's past as a thriving seafood processing center. Today the town has many tourists retracing the steps of those watermen of yesterday. If you would like to see how a yachting center, complete with a 30-ton travel lift and 60-ton railway, handles the needs of today, the best way to view it is from the Dry Dock Restaurant located in the boat yard of Zahniser's yachting center.

My visit was rewarded with the flounder and crab florentine. Here fresh flounder was poached in white wine and wrapped around spinach, stuffed with crab, topped with hollandaise sauce, and served over rice. The results were incredible.

It's all here—fine food and drink with a spectacular view. You will also enjoy the restaurant's impressive collection of antique decoys. Because Dry Dock is very popular, the management suggests that you make a reservation if you plan to come on the weekend.

PIER 1 RESTAURANT

Main Street
Solomons, Maryland
301 / 326-3261

Business Season: all year

Hours: Monday through Saturday—11 AM to 10 PM, Sunday—12 noon to 9 PM

Waterview: Back Creek / Patuxent River

Credit Cards: Diners Club, Visa, MasterCard, Choice

House Specialties: stuffed flounder, shrimp scampi, broiled scallops, crab imperial, crab cakes

The owners of Pier 1 invite you to come see their new establishment and sample their seafood. The old building was destroyed by fire on December 20, 1985.

The rich maritime history of the Chesapeake Bay comes alive in Solomons. Here you can browse through some of the oldest homes in Maryland. Hike along the nearby Calvert Cliffs State Park, a 1,600 acre woodland formed over 15 million years ago, where you will see a rich diversity of life. These cliffs contain more than 600 species of fossils. Also of local interest is the Calvert Marine Museum and Lighthouse, where outdoor exhibits include a boat basin and a recreated salt marsh.

Board the William B. Tennison, built in 1899, for a cruise around Solomons. Visit the restored Drum Point Lighthouse, one of the last of its kind on the Chesapeake. Nearby, the J.D. Lore Oyster House features a boat building exhibit and artifacts of the local seafood industry.

THE NAUGHTY GULL

499 Lore Street
Solomons, Maryland
301 / 326-4855

Business Season: all year

Hours: open daily—11 AM to 12 PM

Waterview: Back Creek / Patuxent River

Credit Cards: Visa and MasterCard

House Specialties: crab cake platter, shrimp scampi, surf 'n' turf, stuffed shrimp, crab imperial, steamed shrimp, fish of the day

More than 50 rivers run into the Chesapeake Bay, the largest estuary in North America. The Patuxent is one of them. In Indian language, "patuxent" means "the place where tobacco grows." One of the little creeks that is a small part of these lovely rivers is home to the Naughty Gull Restaurant. In a cove shaded by pine trees sits this seafood restaurant and pub. On my last visit, the waterside deck off Back Creek had been enclosed. I liked my crab cake and ice cold Bass Ale. I can't wait to return.

THE MARYLAND WAY RESTAURANT
Route 2-4
Solomons Maryland
301 / 326-6311

Business Season: all year

Hours: open daily— breakfast, lunch, and dinner

Waterview: Back Creek / Patuxent River

Credit Cards: American Express, Diners Club, Carte Blanche, Visa, MasterCard, Discover

House Specialties: crab cakes, broiled shrimp, seafood Norfolk, crab soup, oysters on the half shell, oysters casino, oysters Rockefeller, spiced shrimp in the shell

"Famed for its oystering and fishing, historic Solomons Island stretches toward the Chesapeake Bay on Maryland's southwestern shore," a sales brochure tells us. You will find there many lovely restaurants and shops. The Maryland Way Restaurant is part of the Solomons Holiday Inn Hotel, Conference Center, and Marina.

Why not try the Hot Sampler—oysters casino, oysters Rockefeller, clams casino, clams Rockefeller, and mussels. Another excellent choice is the "Maryland Way Steam Pot"—steamed whole lobster, oysters, clams, mussels, and shrimp, served with butter.

VERA'S WHITE SANDS
White Sands Drive
Lusby, Maryland
301 / 586-1182

Business Season: May to December

Hours: Tuesday through Saturday—5 PM to 9 PM, Sunday
1 PM to 9 PM

Waterview: St. Jerome's Creek / Patuxent River

Credit Cards: MasterCard, Visa, Choice

House Specialties: stuffed shrimp, crab and shrimp thermidor,
crab imperial, catch of the day, bouillabaisse

Oh, there are white sands at Vera's, but there is also much, much
more. The brainstorm of owner Vera Freeman, the surroundings look like
the set of a Hollywood studio. The thatched room is jammed full with
treasures that Vera has brought back from her travels around the world:
beaded room dividers, banana trees, leopard-skin bar stools, giant clam
shells, carved elephants inlaid with ivory, mu-mu's, Hawaiian leis, ferns,
flowers, even a tropical rain forest. Bamboo and rattan are in every corner.

Vera's seafood special is bouillabaisse. If you haven't tried the east
coast version of this masterful treat, then you are in for a surprise—shrimp,
scallops, filet of fish, crab, clams, and mussels served in a tomato and wine
sauce. Truly a dish worthy of the gods!

GATSBY'S DOCKSIDE GALLEY
Oyster House Road
Broomes Island, Maryland
301 / 586-2437

Business Season: all year

Hours: Monday—closed, Tuesday through Friday—8 AM to 7 PM, Saturday and Sunday—8 AM to 8 PM

Waterview: Island Creek/Patuxent River

Credit Cards: none

House Specialties: crab cake, soft shell crabs, fried oysters, clam chowder, cream of crab soup, seafood salad

The restaurant got its name from owner Jack Vaughan's boat, The Gatsby, and from Captain Jack's affection for writer F. Scott Fitzgerald. It seems that Jack and his wife, Dorothy, were looking for a boat to buy and ended up buying the restaurant as well. Dorothy was a professional caterer, and Jack had worked as a yacht chef for 8 years, so they were well prepared. This small restaurant is decorated with hats and foul weather yellow slickers, all from past duties that the Captain has held in ships around the world.

The August 1984 issue of *Chesapeake Bay Magazine* reported that "the area around Broomes Island was first acquired by a member of the Broome family in the 17th or early 18th century, according to historian Charles Francis Stern. He writes that the fishing settlement was established after the Civil War by Nathaniel Broome who cut the timber and sold residential lots." Today the seafood industry is alive and well in Calvert County, and fresh seafood is readily available in season. From September to March you can see working oyster boats at Broomes Island.

SANDGATES INN
Sandgates Road
Mechanicsville, Maryland
301 / 373-5100

Business Season: all year

Hours: open daily—10 AM to 10 PM

Waterview: Patuxent River

Credit Cards: none

House Specialties: soft shell crabs, crab cakes, steamed crabs, fried oysters, oyster stew, oysters on the half shell, steamed oysters, crab soup, seafood chowder

Oysters on the half shell, steamed or in a stew. . . just a few of the treats that Sandgates offers you. Others are the soft shell crab sandwich, the steamed crabs, and the seafood chowder plus the wonderful view.

Early photographs reveal that this location had one of the prettiest beaches on the Patuxent. Around 1938 a private home was converted into a restaurant, and it has continued to grow ever since. An old side porch has been glass-enclosed, and three large rooms are open but divided. Another side room has been designated as a game room, offering a pool table, video games, and dart board.

Owners David and Sissie Buckler welcome you to dine at Sandgates, where the relaxing atmosphere and decor will enhance your meal.

DRIFT INN SEAFOOD
Drift Inn Road
Oraville, Maryland
301 / 884-3470

Business Season: May to November

Hours: Friday—5 PM to 9 PM, Saturday—2:30 PM to 10 PM, Sunday—1 PM to 10 PM

Waterview: Patuxent River

Credit Cards: none

House Specialties: steamed crabs, fresh oysters, soft shell crabs

Leonard Copsey opens his inn only 3 days a week and only during certain months, but his method of preparing crabs is one of the best the Bay has to offer. His oysters are wonderful too. Oh, he also serves a few hamburgers and hot dogs. He offers fresh crabs from April to November. From November to April, the Drift Inn becomes an oyster packaging plant. Speaking of oysters, did you know?—the American oyster is a prized seafood delicacy long identified with the Chesapeake Bay area. It was a staple item in the diets of coastal Indians and early settlers. Oysters are graded according to size with the smaller ones going to soups and such and the larger ones being used for breading or for the raw bar.

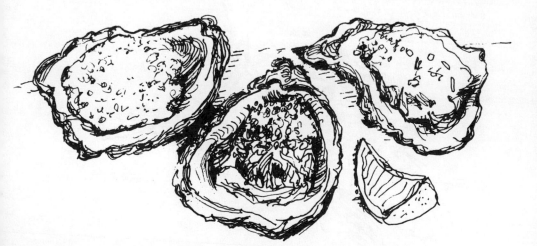

CHAPPELEAR'S RESTAURANT

Patuxent Avenue
Benedict, Maryland
301 / 274-9828

Business Season: all year

Hours: Sunday through Thursday—11 AM to 8 PM, Friday and Saturday—12 noon to 8:45 PM, closed Christmas

Waterview: Patuxent River

Credit Cards: none

House Specialties: crab cake, crab soup, fresh trout sandwich, oysters on the half shell, oysters steamed, oyster stew

When I want a good fish sandwich, I head down to Chappelear's. Owners Francis and Katherine Chappelear take great pride in their restaurant and it shows. Hurricane Hazel wiped out their first location. Francis is a waterman who features his daily catch. Many of the locals come for meals or to purchase the freshly caught oysters.

Chappelear's is a tiny place, but don't pass it by. The rear porch, which sits out over the water, can seat 36. A smaller inside room seats 28. The menu says that all dinners include two vegetables, hot rolls with butter, and salad, but for a special treat, choose one of the fish sandwiches or the seafood platter.

SHORTER'S PLACE

Patuxent Avenue
Benedict, Maryland
301 / 274-3284

Business Season: all year

Hours: open daily—11 AM to 9 PM

Waterview: Patuxent River

Credit Cards: MasterCard, Visa, Discover

House Specialties: combination seafood platter, steamed oysters, crab cakes, fried oysters

One adventure in the Patuxent River area is a visit to the ancient Battle Creek Cypress Swamp, a gray-brown world of towering cypress trees. It provides a rare view of the swampy southern world in one of its northernmost locations. Another adventure is a visit to Shorter's Place.

Shorter's, one of southern Maryland's oldest and most established restaurants, has served fine seafood since 1930. Today it is run by third and fourth generation owners Harry and Roy Shorter, father and son. The entrance way and cozy pine-paneled dining room are decorated with oil paintings of waterfront scenes. From our seats through high windows, we watched the crabbers on the pier.

You may want to order the Patuxent oysters, fried in an old-time secret recipe batter. Another good choice is the combination seafood platter that includes liberal portions of fish, shrimp, scallops, crab cakes, oysters, crab or shrimp salad, hush puppies, french fries, cole slaw, and tossed salad.

After your meal, enjoy looking at the historic town. According to a road sign I spotted, Benedict was "founded in 1683 as Benedict-Leonard town. Here a vessel was constructed for George Washington in 1760. In 1814, British troops under General Ross landed nearby for their march to the city of Washington."

RAY'S PIER RESTAURANT
DeSoto Landing Road
Benedict, Maryland
301 / 274-3733

Business Season: all year

Hours: Tuesday through Thursday—11 AM to 8 PM, Friday and Saturday—11 AM to 9 PM, Sunday—11 AM to 8 PM

Waterview: Patuxent River

Credit Cards: none

House Specialties: steamed shrimp, fried shrimp, fried oysters, crab cakes, scallops, seafood platter, steak and seafood combination platter, catch of the day, shrimp cocktail, oyster stew

You will find Ray's Pier, a large white building, at the end of DeSoto Landing Road at the water's edge. You enter through a side door that opens to a long friendly bar. The day we arrived the bar area was full so we eased our way to the refreshing dining room.

The large windows reaching from floor to ceiling offered a view of the Patuxent River bridge and midday traffic. The river was almost frozen over and we watched the many cardinals, ducks, gulls, and Baltimore orioles in the small garden; they were enjoying the corn that owners Ray and Pat Rawlings had placed there for winter feedings.

Traditional Bay Sampler Recipes

Clam Sampler

Steamed Clams in Wine Broth

48 clams
½ cup dry white wine
2 tablespoons butter
1 stick butter, melted
fresh lemon

Scrub clams thoroughly with a brush under cold running water. Using a large pan with a rack, pour in wine and add the 2 tablespoons butter. Arrange scrubbed clams on the rack. Cover and steam just until the shells open, about 6 to 10 minutes. Use melted butter for dipping, use lemon for sprinkling. Serves 6.

Clam Fritters

1 pint clams
1¾ cups all-purpose flour
1 tablespoon baking powder
1 teaspoon chopped parsley
1½ teaspoons salt
2 eggs, beaten
1 cup milk
2 teaspoons grated onion
1 tablespoon butter

Drain clams and chop. Combine dry ingredients. Combine eggs, milk, onion, butter, and clams. Combine with dry ingredients and stir until smooth. Drop batter by teaspoonsful into hot shortening at 350 °F and fry for 3 minutes, or until golden brown. Drain on absorbent paper. Serves 4.

Clams Casino

24 clams on the half shell,
  arranged on beds of rock salt

1 stick butter, softened

½ cup each chopped shallots,
  parsley and green pepper

2 tablespoons lemon juice

1 teaspoon salt

freshly ground pepper

6 strips bacon, partially broiled

Saute peppers, parsley and shallots until soft, add salt and pepper and cover the clams with the cooked mixture, squeeze lemon juice over clams and top with bacon. Broil until bacon is crisp. Serves 4.

Fried Soft Shell Clams

1 to 2 cups pancake mix
  (regular or buttermilk)

36 shucked soft shell clams, chopped

peanut oil for frying

salt

Put pancake mix into large shallow bowl. Add a handful of clams and toss lightly with both hands until well coated. Shake off excess breading in wire basket.

Deep fry in oil at 375 °F for 1½ to 2 minutes. Drain on absorbent paper.

Repeat process until all clams are cooked. Salt lightly and serve at once. Serves 4.

Clam Chowder

¼ pound salt pork
2 large onions, chopped
1 carrot, diced
1 cup chopped celery
1 green pepper, diced
2 cups cooked tomatoes
4 cups water
thyme
salt and pepper
2 dozen large clams,
    shucked and minced
crackers

Dice salt pork, brown and remove cracklings from fat. Brown onions, carrot, celery and green pepper lightly in the fat. Add tomatoes, water, seasonings and clams. Cook over low heat for 30 minutes. Serve with crackers. Serves 6.

Clam Chowder

24 clams
¼ cup chopped bacon
¼ cup chopped onion
2 cups clam liquor and water
1 cup diced potatoes
½ teaspoon salt
dash pepper
2 cups milk
parsley

Drain clams and save liquor. Chop. Fry bacon until lightly brown. Add onion and cook until tender. Add liquor and water, potatoes, seasonings, and clams. Cook about 15 minutes or until potatoes are tender. Add milk; heat. Garnish with chopped parsley sprinkled over the top. Serves 6.

Steamed Clams

48 clams
salt and pepper, for sprinkling
seafood seasoning, for sprinkling
½ cup water
melted butter

Wash clams thoroughly. Place in pan. Sprinkle lightly with seasonings. Add water, cover tightly, and bring to boiling point. Reduce heat and steam 10 to 15 minutes or until shells open wide. Drain clams, reserving liquid. Strain liquid.

Serve clams hot in shells with separate containers of clam liquid and melted butter for dunking. Serves 6.

Cioppino

1 cup sliced celery

1 cup chopped green pepper

2 large onions, chopped

2 large cloves garlic, minced

½ cup olive oil

4 cups vegetable juice cocktail

2 cups chicken stock or broth

1 cup dry red wine

1 cup dry white wine

¼ cup tomato sauce

1 large bay leaf

1 teaspoon basil, crushed

2 dried red chilies, chopped

½ teaspoon sugar

2 pounds fish filets,
  cut in 2-inch pieces

1 pound shrimp, shelled and deveined

2 dozen cherrystone clams, scrubbed

½ cup chopped parsley

In large deep saucepan or Dutch oven, saute celery, green pepper, onion and garlic in oil until vegetables are tender. Add juice, chicken broth, wines, tomato sauce, bay leaf, basil, chilies and sugar. Simmer 30 minutes. Add fish and shrimp. Cook 5 minutes. Add clams; cook just until shells open. Ladle into soup bowls. Garnish with parsley. Serves 8.

Crab Sampler

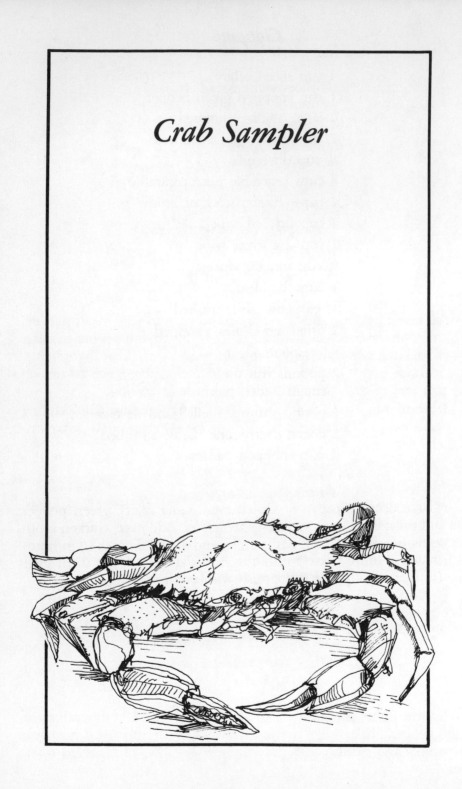

Crab Cakes

1½ slices white bread, crust
    removed and diced

⅓ cup milk

1 pound crab meat

1 teaspoon fresh parsley, minced

1 teaspoon onion, minced

2 tablespoons mayonnaise

½ teaspoon worcestershire sauce

½ teaspoon salt

freshly ground pepper

4 tablespoons butter

Soak bread pieces in milk for a few minutes. Add crab meat, parsley, onion, mayonnaise and worcestershire sauce. Add salt and pepper to taste. Mix well, making sure crab meat is well integrated with other ingredients. Shape mixture into 8 patties, each about 1 inch thick. Place patties on a flat pan and chill in the refrigerator for at least an hour.

Melt butter in a large, heavy skillet until gently sizzling. Cook chilled crab cakes about 4 to 5 minutes to a side, browning them well. Serve immediately. Serves 4.

Crab Meat Norfolk

2 tablespoons butter

juice of half lemon

1 pound crab meat

salt and pepper to taste

paprika

2 tablespoons minced parsley

4 slices buttered toast

Heat the butter and juice of half a lemon in skillet. Add the crab meat, salt and pepper. Shake skillet to mingle flavors. When mixture is hot, dust with paprika and garnish with parsley. Serve on slices of buttered toast. Serves 4.

Fried Soft Shell Crabs

12 cleaned soft crabs
salt and pepper
flour
butter and oil for frying

Dry crabs with paper towel. Sprinkle with salt and pepper. Lightly coat with flour. Cook crabs in fry pan, in just enough oil and butter mixture to prevent sticking, until browned; about 5 minutes on each side. Serves 6.

Crab Casserole

¼ cup butter, melted
¼ cup flour
2 teaspoons salt
⅛ teaspoon pepper
1 teaspoon paprika
1 teaspoon minced onion
3¼ cups milk
1 pound crab meat
⅓ cup dry sherry
1¼ cup macaroni shells,
  cooked and drained
1 8½-ounce can artichoke
  hearts, drained
¼ cup grated sharp cheddar
  cheese

Remove butter from heat; stir in flour, salt, pepper and paprika until smooth. Add onion; stir in milk gradually; bring to boil. Reduce heat; simmer for 5 minutes. Combine crab meat, sherry, macaroni and artichoke hearts with sauce; place in 2½-quart casserole. Sprinkle with cheese. Bake in 350°F oven for about 20 minutes. Serves 6.

Crab Quiche

1 partially baked 9-inch pastry shell
1 pound crab meat
2 tablespoons finely chopped shallots
2 tablespoons butter
2 tablespoons finely chopped parsley
1 teaspoon finely chopped tarragon

2 tablespoons wine
4 eggs
1 to 1½ cups heavy cream
salt and pepper
¼ cup grated Parmesan cheese

Simmer the chopped shallots in the butter for just a few minutes, until they are soft, but not brown. put crab meat in a mixing bowl, keeping pieces as large as possible; add shallots, parsley, tarragon, and wine. In a separate bowl, beat together the eggs and cream, then gently fold into the crab meat mixture. Season with salt and pepper. Pour into the pastry shell, sprinkle with Parmesan cheese, and bake in 350 °F oven until custard is set about 30 minutes. Serve hot. Serves 4.

Crab Imperial

3 eggs

4 tablespoons mayonnaise

2 tablespoons dry white wine

2 tablespoons sweet pickle relish

1 teaspoon dill weed

2 teaspoons seafood seasoning

1 pound lump backfin crab meat

In a bowl, whip the eggs until fluffy. Beat in the mayonnaise, and wine. Add the pickle relish, dill weed and seafood seasoning and mix well. Gently fold in the crab meat, then spoon the mixture into buttered individual dishes. Bake at 375 °F for 20 to 25 minutes or until lightly golden on top. Serves 4.

Imperial Crab

1 pound crab meat

2 tablespoons chopped onion

2 tablespoons chopped green pepper

3 tablespoons butter

2 tablespoons flour

½ cup milk

½ teaspoon salt

dash pepper

¼ teaspoon worcestershire sauce

2 hard-cooked eggs, chopped

Remove any shell or cartilage from crab meat, being careful not to break the meat into small pieces. Cook onion and green pepper in butter until tender. Blend in flour. Add milk gradually and cook until thick, stirring constantly. Add seasonings, egg, and crab meat. Place in 6 well-greased, individual shells. Bake in a moderate oven, 350 °F, for 20 to 25 minutes or until golden brown. Serves 6.

Crab Au Gratin

1 pound crab meat
2 tablespoons butter, melted
salt and pepper to taste
½ cup cream or evaporated milk
2 egg yolks, well beaten
½ cup grated cheese

Combine butter, crab meat, salt and pepper; cook for 5 minutes without browning. Mix cream with egg yolks; add to hot crab meat mixture. Cook for 4 minutes over low heat, stirring constantly. Pour into large casserole; sprinkle cheese over top. Bake in 350 °F oven until cheese is melted. Serves 4.

Crab Louis Salad

½ cup mayonnaise
½ cup chili sauce
2 tablespoons chopped green pepper
2 tablespoons chopped sweet pickle
1 tablespoon chopped onion
1 tablespoon lemon juice
1 pound lump crab meat
lettuce
2 tomatoes, quartered
2 green peppers, sliced
2 hard-cooked eggs, diced
pimiento strips

Combine mayonnaise, chili sauce, chopped green pepper, sweet pickle, onion, and lemon juice; blend well. Add crab meat, tossing lightly. Chill thoroughly.

At serving time, spoon salad on lettuce. Garnish with tomatoes, green pepper slices, eggs, and pimiento. Serves 4.

Deviled Crab

1 pound crab meat

2 tablespoons chopped onion

1 clove garlic, minced

3 tablespoons butter

2 tablespoons flour

¾ cup milk

½ teaspoon salt

dash pepper

½ teaspoon dry mustard

1 teaspoon worcestershire sauce

½ teaspoon sage

dash cayenne pepper

1 tablespoon lemon juice

1 egg, beaten

1 tablespoon chopped parsley

Remove any shell or cartilage from crab meat. Cook onion and garlic in butter until tender. Blend in flour. Add milk gradually and cook until thick, stirring constantly. Add seasonings and lemon juice. Stir a little of the hot sauce into egg; add to remaining sauce, stirring constantly. Add parsley and crab meat. Place in 6 well-greased, individual shells. Bake in a moderate oven, 350 °F, for 15 to 20 minutes or until brown. Serves 6.

Baked Crab in Shells

1 pound crab meat
½ cup chopped onion
¼ cup butter
2 tablespoons flour
½ cup milk
½ cup tomato sauce
½ teaspoon salt
dash pepper
¼ cup grated cheese
½ cup soft bread crumbs

Remove any shell or cartilage from crab meat. Cook onion in butter until tender. Blend in flour. Add milk gradually and cook until thick, stirring constantly. Add tomato sauce, seasonings, and crab meat. Place in 6 well-greased, individual shells or 5-ounce custard cups. Combine cheese and crumbs; sprinkle over top of each shell. Bake in a moderate oven, 350 °F, for 20 to 25 minutes or until brown. Serves 6.

Broiled Crab Meat in Shells

1 pound crab meat
⅓ cup butter
2 tablespoons lemon juice
¼ teaspoon salt
dash cayenne pepper
chopped parsley

Remove any shell or cartilage from crab meat. Combine butter, lemon juice, salt, cayenne pepper, and crab meat. Place in 6 well-greased, individual shells or 5-ounce custard cups. Place on a broiler pan about 4 inches from source of heat. Broil for 7 to 10 minutes or until brown. Garnish with parsley sprinkled over top of each shell. Serves 6.

She Crab Soup

1 pound crab meat
　with crab eggs

2 tablespoons butter

2 medium yellow onions, minced

1 tablespoon flour

1 quart hot milk

salt and pepper to taste

pinch nutmeg

4 ounces dry sherry

8 ounces heavy cream

Melt the butter in a large skillet and saute the onions until they are soft. Add the crab meat and crab eggs. Saute for a few seconds. Sprinkle the flour over the crab mixture and stir until the flour blends with the butter. Add the hot milk gradually, stirring constantly.

Simmer very slowly for 20 minutes. Season with salt, pepper and nutmeg. Add the sherry and cream. Heat to just below the boiling point. Serves 6.

Cream of Crab Soup

1 pound lump crab meat

1 pint of milk

1 pint of cream

½ stick of butter

2 tablespoons of sherry

½ teaspoon ground mace

2 pieces of lemon peel

¼ cup of cracker crumbs

salt and pepper to taste

Put milk in top of double boiler with mace and lemon peel and allow to simmer for a few minutes. Then add crab, butter and cream and cook for 15 minutes. Thicken with cracker crumbs. Season with salt and pepper. Just before serving, add sherry. Serves 6.

Crab Soup

1 pound crab meat
1 large can tomatoes
6 potatoes, diced
2 medium onions, diced
2 cups whole kernel corn
1 cup lima beans
1 cup green beans
2 stalks celery, diced
2 carrots, diced
¼ cup chopped parsley
water
2 tablespoons mustard
salt to taste
2 tablespoons
   Old Bay Seasoning to taste

Combine crab meat, water and Old Bay Seasoning. Simmer about 30 minutes. Add remaining seasonings and vegetables and simmer until vegetables are tender. Serves 10.

Steamed Crabs

one dozen crabs
2½ tablespoons Old Bay Seasoning
3 tablespoons salt
water and vinegar

Pot should have raised rack, minimum 2 inches high. Add equal quantities vinegar and water to just below level of rack. Layer crabs; sprinkle each layer with mixture of salt and Old Bay Seasoning. Cover and steam until crabs are red.

Crab Newburg

1 pound crab meat
⅓ cup butter
3 tablespoons flour
½ teaspoon salt
½ teaspoon paprika
dash cayenne pepper
1½ cups coffee cream
3 egg yolks
2 tablespoons sherry
toast points

Remove any shell or cartilage from crab meat, being careful not to break the meat into small pieces. Melt butter; blend in flour and seasonings. Add cream gradually and cook until thick and smooth, stirring constantly. Stir a little of the hot sauce into egg yolk; add to remaining sauce, stirring constantly. Add crab meat; heat. Remove from heat and slowly stir in sherry. Serve immediately on toast points. Serves 6.

Fried Stuffed Hard Crab

12 steamed hard crabs

3 cups crab cake mix

6 cups pancake mix

4 teaspoons Old Bay Seasoning

3 to 4 cups milk

peanut oil for deep frying

Remove apron, top shell, fat and gills from crabs. Firmly pack about ¼ cup crab cake mixture into top cavity of each crab.

Put pancake mix and seafood seasoning in large bowl. Stir in milk until mixture is consistency of thick pancake batter.

Dip crabs into batter, one at a time, making sure to coat all sides well. Lift crab by large claw and let excess batter drain off. Put in wire basket and deep fry at 375 °F until golden brown, 3 to 4 minutes. Drain. Serve at once. Serves 12.

Crab Cake Mix

1 pound crab meat

2 tablespoons butter

1 tablespoon green pepper, chopped

1 tablespoon onion, chopped

½ cup mayonnaise

dash hot sauce

Pick through crab meat and set aside, melt butter and saute pepper and onion until soft and clear. Combine all and use as stuffing.

Crab Casserole

1 cup celery, chopped

8 slices soft white bread,
  crusts removed, diced

1 pound crab meat

1 onion, chopped

½ cup mayonnaise

½ cup green pepper, chopped

½ cup slivered blanched almonds

4 eggs, beaten

3 cups milk

1 cup undiluted canned cream of
  mushroom soup (condensed)

grated Parmesan cheese

paprika

Cook celery slowly for 10 minutes in a little water; drain. Spread half the diced bread evenly in a greased 2-quart souffle dish. Mix in a large bowl the crab meat, onion, mayonnaise, green pepper, half the almonds and the celery. Spread crab mixture evenly over the bread. On top of this filling place the remaining diced bread. Beat eggs, milk and soup together and pour over the contents in the dish. Top with Parmesan cheese, paprika and remaining almonds. Serves 6.

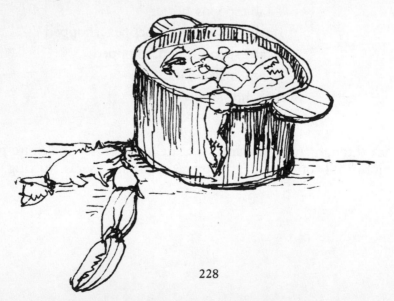

Crab Salad

1 pound crab meat
¾ cup chopped celery (2 to 3 stalks)
2 tablespoons lemon juice
1 teaspoon salt
⅛ teaspoon pepper
3 tablespoons mayonnaise
1 teaspoon capers

Remove all cartilage from crab meat. Put celery in bowl. Mix in lemon juice, salt, pepper, mayonnaise and capers. Add crab meat and mix gently but thoroughly. Serves 4.

Crab Cocktail

1 pound crab meat
lettuce
cocktail sauce
parsley
lemon wedges

Remove any shell or cartilage from crab meat, being careful not to break the meat into small pieces. Arrange lettuce in 6 cocktail glasses. Place crab meat on top; cover with cocktail sauce. Garnish with parsley and lemon wedges. Serves 6.

Cocktail Sauce

¾ cup catsup
¼ cup lemon juice
3 tablespoons chopped celery
½ teaspoon salt
6 drops tobasco
dash cayenne pepper

Combine all ingredients and chill.

Fish Sampler

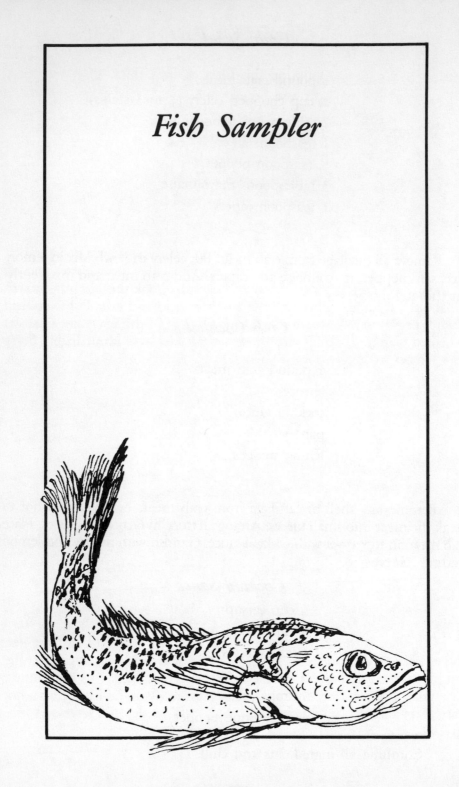

Sauteed Sea Trout

1 pound fish filets, ½ inch thick
salt and pepper
flour
1 tablespoon butter
1 tablespoon olive oil
chopped parsley or dill
lemon wedges for garnish

Pat fish dry with paper towels. Season lightly with salt and pepper. Coat fish with flour; shake off excess. In wide skillet, heat butter and oil on medium-high heat until it foams. Add fish. Cook until lightly browned, about 2 minutes. Turn carefully and brown second side. Fish is cooked when it begins to flake when tested with a fork at its thickest point. Transfer to heated platter. Sprinkle with parsley or dill and serve immediately. Serve with lemon wedges. Serves 4.

Flounder Almondine

2 pounds fresh flounder filets
1 teaspoon salt
dash pepper
1 cup flour
½ cup butter
½ cup blanched slivered almonds
2 tablespoons chopped parsley

Cut filets into serving-size portions. Sprinkle with salt and pepper. Roll in flour. Fry in butter. When fish is brown on one side, turn carefully and brown the other side. Cooking time is approximately 7 to 10 minutes, depending on thickness of fish. Remove fish from pan and place on a hot platter. Fry almonds until lightly browned. Add parsley and serve over fish. Serves 6.

Broiled Fish

1 pound fish filets, ¾ to 1½ inches
salt and pepper
herbs: chopped parsley, dried
    thyme, marjoram, basil, tarragon
    or winter savory
1 tablespoon melted butter
1 tablespoon fresh lemon juice
lemon wedges for garnish

Lightly grease broiler pan. Pat fish dry with paper towels. Season lightly with salt, pepper and / or choice of herbs. Arrange on broiler pan without crowding. Combine butter and lemon juice to make basting sauce; brush on fish. Broil 4 to 5 inches from source of heat, turning and basting once, until fish is light brown and begins to flake when tested with a fork but is still moist; allow 10 minutes per inch thickness measured at its thickest point. Transfer fish to warm serving platter. Serve with lemon wedges. Serves 4.

Fried Fish

½ pound pan dressed
    fish filets, per person
salt, pepper for sprinkling
lemon for sprinkling
1 to 2 cups dry pancake mix
peanut oil for frying
cocktail or tartar sauce

Wash and dry fish. Dip fish into clean, cool water, sprinkle lightly with salt and lemon and pepper seasoning; then coat lightly with pancake mix.

Fry in deep fat at 350 °F for 4 to 5 minutes, or fry in 1½ inches hot fat in fry pan, 4 to 5 minuts on each side. (Fish is done when browned on both sides and flakes easily when tested with a fork. Be careful not to overcook.)

Remove fish from pan and drain on paper towel. Serve with cocktail or tartar sauce. Serves 4.

Broiled Shad Roe

2 shad roe
salted water
juice of ½ lemon
cold water
4 tablespoons butter
salt and pepper to taste
1 teaspoon white wine vinegar
1 tablespoon chopped parsley
crisp bacon
scrambled eggs

Simmer shad roe 15 minutes in salted water with lemon juice, to cover. Remove with slotted spatula. Transfer to cold water for 5 minutes, drain, and pat dry.

Melt butter in a saucepan, sprinkle roe with salt and pepper, place on a greased rack, and brush surface with butter. Broil approximately 4 inches from flame for 5 minutes. Turn, and again brush with butter.

Broil until surface is a light golden brown. Place on serving platter or plates. Cook remaining butter in saucepan over high heat until it turns quite dark. Stir in vinegar and parsley. Pour over shad roe and serve with crisp bacon and scrambled eggs. Serves 2.

Simple Stuffed Flounder

1 pound flounder
8 ounces crab meat
½ cup Ritz cracker crumbs
2 tablespoons melted butter
½ teaspoon salt
½ teaspoon pepper
thick white sauce

Mix crab meat, buttered crumbs, salt and pepper in a bowl. Lay fish flat. Spread mixture on top, then roll filets like a jelly roll. Place roll in a shallow baking dish lined with butter, then pour white sauce over fish. Cover and bake at 350°F for 15-20 minutes. Serves 4.

White Sauce

4 tablespoons butter
4 tablespoons all-purpose flour
salt and freshly ground white
    pepper to taste
1 cup dry white wine
1 cup cream

Melt butter in heavy saucepan over low heat. Stir in flour to make a roux. Add salt and pepper. Keep heat low so roux will not turn brown (or burn) and stir constantly so it will not stick to the pan. Cook for several minutes.

Slowly stir in wine. Add cream at this point to make a richer sauce. Do not overheat sauce, or cream may curdle. Cook, stirring, until sauce is smooth and creamy. Yields 2 cups.

Baked Fish

1 pound fish filets, ¾ to 1½
    inches thick, cut into serving
  size pieces

2 tablespoons cornmeal

2 tablespoons flour

¼ teaspoon paprika
  salt and pepper

1 tablespoon oil

1 tablespoon grated Parmesan cheese

Pat fish dry with paper towels. Combine cornmeal, flour, paprika and dash each salt and pepper in flat dish. Place oil in baking dish; heat in 425 °F oven 1 minute. Dredge fish in cornmeal mixture; shake off excess. Place in baking dish and turn to coat with oil. Arrange fish pieces 1-inch apart. Sprinkle with Parmesan cheese. Bake at 425 °F allowing 10 minutes per inch thickness measured at its thickest part. Fish flakes when tested with a fork. Serve with your choice of sauce. Serves 4.

Sauteed Flounder

1 tablespoon oil

1 tablespoon butter

1 pound flounder

1 tablespoon lemon juice

1 tablespoon chopped parsley

Saute flounder in oil and butter for 10 minutes per inch of thickness measured at the thickest part of the fish, turning once halfway through cooking time. Remove to warm platter. Mix lemon juice and parsley with pan juices and pour over fish. Serves 4.

Mussels and Scallops Sampler

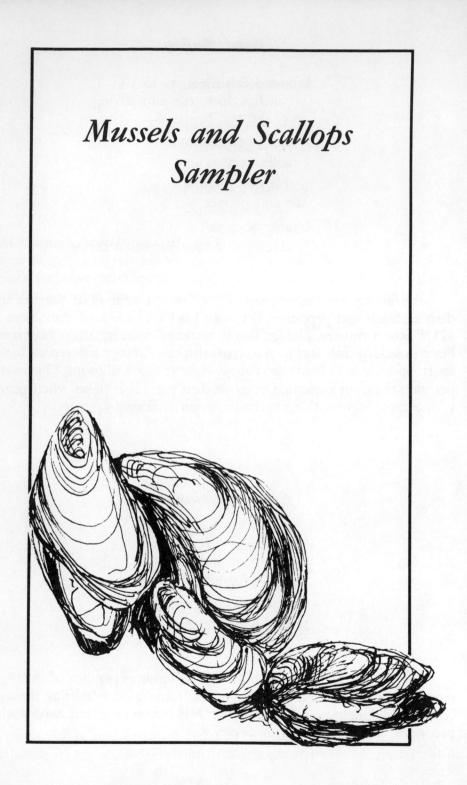

Steamed Mussels

36 mussels, washed
½ cup water
½ cup dry white wine
¼ cup minced parsley
4 cloves garlic, minced
freshly ground black pepper

Place mussels in a 4-quart saucepan. Add water, wine, parsley, and garlic. Cover pan and place over high heat. Shake the pan once or twice during cooking. When mussels have opened, they are done. Remove mussels from pan and place in heated bowls. Strain hot broth and pour over mussels. Sprinkle mussels with pepper and serve. Serves 4.

Bouillabaisse

½ dozen cherrystone clams in shell
½ dozen oysters
½ cup crab meat
1 dozen mussels in shell
½ pound filet of flounder
2 tablespoons butter
1 8-ounce can tomato sauce
½ cup water
2 tablespoons basil
bay leaf
dash worcestershire sauce
½ cup white wine
¼ teaspoon salt
⅛ teaspoon pepper
½ teaspoon paprika

Scrub the shellfish. Cut the flounder in pieces and gently saute it in the butter. Add everything else and simmer, covered, for 20 minutes. Serves 4.

Mussels in Herb Butter

2 dozen mussels

½ cup softened butter

1 tablespoon chopped parsley

1 tablespoon sweet marjoram

1 tablespoon lemon juice

3 shallots

3 large cloves garlic

1 slice raw bacon, minced

salt and pepper

Steam well-scrubbed mussels open. Save half a shell for each mussel. Blend the remaining ingredients thoroughly. Put small amount of herb butter in each shell. Lay mussel on it. Cover with more butter and place them in single layer in shallow pans (pie tins). Heat oven to 400 °F and bake for 15 to 20 minutes. Serves 4.

Baked Scallops

1 pound fresh bay scallops

1 cup water

½ cup dry white wine

3 tablespoons butter

3 tablespoons flour

½ teaspoon salt

¼ teaspoon paprika

¼ cup shredded cheddar cheese

1 cup grated carrots

¼ teaspoon mustard

2 tablespoons melted butter

1 cup soft fresh bread crumbs

Poach the scallops in softly simmering water and wine for 2 minutes. Remove scallops to warm place and save all liquids. Melt 3 tablespoons of butter, stir in flour, salt and paprika. Add reserved hot liquid and cook, stirring until thickened and bubbly. Add cheese, grated carrots, and mustard. Cook over low heat until cheese is melted. Add scallops. Turn into 4 baking shells. Sprinkle buttered bread crumbs over and bake in 400 °F oven for 5 minutes. Serves 4.

Scallops Newburg

1 pound bay scallops
2 tablespoons butter
¼ cup sherry
3 egg yolks beaten slightly
½ cup cream
½ teaspoon salt
cayenne

Rinse and drain scallops; cover with cold water. Heat slowly to boiling and drain. Cook scallops in butter 3 minutes, breaking into small pieces as you stir. Add sherry. Cook 1 minute longer.

Mix egg yolks and cream. Add to scallops and cook just until mixture thickens, stirring constantly. Remove from heat immediately. Season with salt and cayenne and serve on toast or crackers. Serves 4.

Fried Scallops

1 cup dry bread crumbs

1 teaspoon salt

½ teaspoon celery salt

1 pound scallops

1 egg

2 tablespoons water

Combine crumbs and seasonings. Dip scallops into crumbs, then into egg diluted with water and dip into crumbs again. Saute or fry in hot deep fat 365 °F 4 to 5 minutes. Serve with tartar sauce. Serves 4.

Bay Scallops with Linguine

12 ounces linguine

3 tablespoons butter

2 tablespoons olive oil

1 medium onion, finely chopped

1 clove garlic, minced

1 large tomato, peeled, seeded
   and chopped

1 pound bay scallops

½ cup dry white wine

¼ cup minced parsley

salt and pepper

Bring plenty of salted water to a boil. Add linguine and cook for the least amount of time suggested on the box.

Heat butter and oil in a skillet. Add onion and garlic and saute for 3 minutes, add tomato, add scallops and cook until they are firm. Add wine, bring to a boil and remove skillet from heat. Stir in the parsley, and salt and pepper. Drain linquini and place in a warm serving bowl. Top with scallop sauce. Serves 4.

Sauteed Scallops

1 pound scallops
1 small onion, minced
2 tablespoons butter
½ teaspoon salt
⅛ teaspoon pepper
parsley

Wash scallops quickly and cook 5 minutes in a small amount of boiling water. Drain and dry. Cook onion in butter until tender. Add scallops and cook until brown. Season and sprinkle with parsley. Serves 4.

Scallops and Rice Au Gratin

1 pound scallops
¼ cup chopped onion
½ cup chopped celery
½ cup chopped green pepper
¼ cup butter, melted
¼ cup all-purpose flour
1 teaspoon salt
dash pepper
1 cup milk
2 cups cooked rice
1 cup shredded cheese

Remove any shell particles and coarsely chop. Cook onion, celery, and green pepper in butter until tender. Blend in flour and seasonings. Add milk gradually and cook until thick, stirring constantly. Add scallops. Place one-half the rice in a well-greased 1½-quart casserole dish, cover with one-half the scallop mixture, and one-half the cheese. Repeat. Bake at 350°F for 25 to 30 minutes, or until brown. Serves 6.

Oyster Sampler

Oysters on the Half Shell

oysters—½ dozen per person
ice
cocktail sauce
lemon
saltines

Wash oysters and chill thoroughly. Open and serve on cracked ice with cocktail sauce and saltines. Use lemon for garnish.

Oysters Rockefeller

48 oysters on half shell
1 bunch spinach
2 bunches green onions
1 stalk celery
1 bunch parsley
1 stick butter melted
1½ cups bread crumbs
3 tablespoons worcestershire sauce
1 tablespoon anchovy paste
salt to taste
hot sauce to taste
2 ounces Pernod
¾ cup bread crumbs

Grind spinach, onion, celery and parsley very fine. Mix in 1 stick butter, melted and 1½ cups bread crumbs. Season with worcestershire sauce, anchovy paste, salt and hot sauce to taste. Add Pernod and mix well. Put oysters in shells which are on rock salt, and cover each with some sauce. Cover with bread crumbs. Bake in 450°F oven until brown. Serve hot. Serves 4.

Fried Oysters

1 pint oysters
2 eggs
1 tablespoon water
1 cup flour
1 teaspoon seafood seasoning
salt and pepper to taste
1 cup bread crumbs or cracker meal
Peanut oil for frying

Drain oysters and pat dry with a paper towel. Beat eggs with water and add salt and pepper to taste. Combine seafood seasoning with flour. Dust each oyster with flour mixture, then dip into the egg batter and roll in crumbs, allow oysters to sit about 10 minutes before frying. Pan fry in shallow peanut oil and turn once. Serves 2.

Oysters Casino

3 slices bacon, chopped
1 small onion, chopped
1 small stalk celery, chopped
1 teaspoon lemon juice
1 teaspoon salt
⅛ teaspoon pepper
6 drops worcestershire sauce
4 drops hot sauce
¼ teaspoon seafood seasoning
36 oysters

Fry bacon until partially cooked. Add onion and celery and cook until tender. Add lemon juice and seasonings.

Arrange oysters in shallow baking pan. Spread bacon mixture over oysters. Bake at 400 °F for 10 minutes or until edges of oysters begin to curl. Serve hot as appetizers. Serves 6.

Oyster Fritters

1 pint shucked oysters
½ cup evaporated milk
1 cup pancake mix
2 tablespoons cornmeal
1 teaspoon salt
¼ teaspoon pepper
¾ cup peanut oil

Drain oysters, reserving liquor. Put oysters in bowl; mix in milk. Add pancake mix, cornmeal, salt and pepper. Mix well. (Batter will be thick.)

Heat oil in fry pan. Drop batter into hot oil by tablespoonsful making sure to include 2 oysters in each portion. Cook until brown on one side, 1 to 2 minutes. Turn carefully and brown the other side. Makes about 18 fritters.

NOTE: If batter becomes to thick on standing, thin with oyster liquor.

Oyster Stew

1 pint oysters
¼ cup melted butter
1 quart milk
1½ teaspoons salt
⅛ teaspoon pepper
paprika
1 teaspoon thyme

Drain oysters, reserving liquor. Remove any remaining shell particles. Add oysters and liquor to butter and cook until edges of oysters begin to curl. Add milk, salt, and pepper; heat thoroughly but do not boil. Garnish with paprika and thyme. Serves 6.

Oyster Pie

1 onion, minced
½ cup minced celery
¼ cup minced green pepper
½ stick butter
1½ tablespoons flour
36 oysters, drained, reserve liquid
¼ cup minced parsley
1½ teaspoons worcestershire
dash hot sauce
½ teaspoon salt
1 recipe plain pastry

Saute onion, celery and pepper in 2 tablespoons butter until soft. Brown flour in remaining 2 tablespoons butter; stir in sauteed mixture. Add oysters and simmer 5 minutes. If mixture is too dry, add small amount oyster liquid. Add parsley, sauces and salt to taste. Pour into unbaked 9-inch pastry shell. Cover with top pastry and make several slits in top. Bake in 400°F oven 20 minutes or until brown. Serves 4.

Steamed Oysters

48 oysters in shell

10 cups water

1 tablespoon worcestershire sauce

2 tablespoons fresh lemon juice

1 stick butter, melted

Wash oysters. Chip excess shell off the end of each oyster.

Place in kettle. Add water, worcestershire sauce, and lemon juice. Put cover on tightly and steam until open. It takes about 15 minutes. Remove top shells and serve on a platter with butter and lemon. Serves 4.

Scalloped Oysters

1 pint oysters

2 cups coarse cracker crumbs

½ cup melted butter

½ teaspoon salt

⅛ teaspoon pepper

¼ teaspoon worcestershire sauce

1 cup milk

Drain oysters. Combine cracker crumbs, butter, salt and pepper. Reserve ⅓ mixture for topping. Place another ⅓ of crumb mixture in a well-greased, 1-quart casserole; cover with a layer of oysters. Repeat layers. Add worcestershire sauce to milk, and pour over contents of casserole. Top with reserved ⅓ crumb mixture. Bake in a moderate oven, 350 °F, for 30 minutes or until thoroughly heated. Serves 6.

Shrimp Sampler

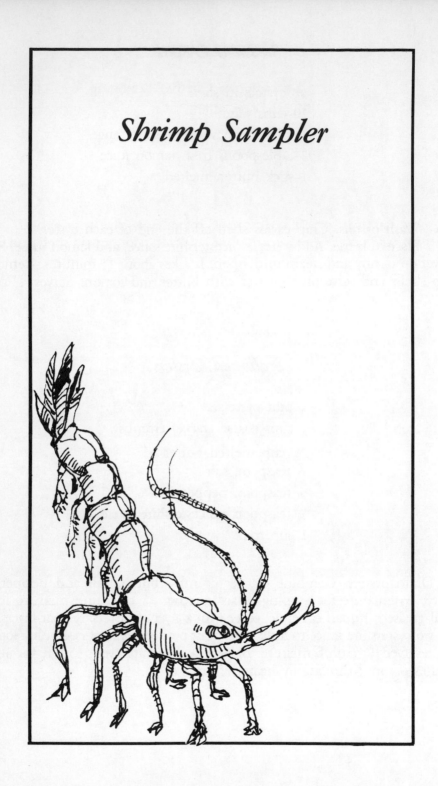

Steamed Shrimp

1 tablespoon Old Bay Seasoning
1 teaspoon salt
½ cup water
½ cup vinegar
1 pound shrimp

In saucepan combine first four ingredients. Bring to a boil. Add shrimp, stir gently. Cover, steam until tender. Drain, remove shell and vein on back.

Shrimp "Scampi"

2 pounds jumbo shrimp, shelled, deveined, tails intact
1 cup olive oil
3 tablespoons dry white wine
2 tablespoons minced parsley
2 cloves garlic, crushed
1 teaspoon salt
several grindings of fresh pepper

Rinse the shrimp in cool water, pat dry. Mix the olive oil, wine, parsley, garlic, salt, and pepper to taste. Pour over the shrimp in a shallow dish. Cover and chill for 2 to 3 hours in the refrigerator, turning the shrimp once or twice in the marinade. Preheat the broiler. Put the shrimp on a foil-lined broiler pan, brush with the marinade, and broil about 6 inches from the heat, 3 minutes to a side, basting with the marinade. Serve immediately with piping hot rice. Serves 6.

Barbecued Shrimp

24 large fresh shrimp, shelled
and deveined (tails intact)

½ cup lemon / lime juice
(well mixed)

¾ cup olive oil

4 medium cloves garlic, chopped

chopped hot peppers

Mix citrus juice, ½ cup olive oil, garlic, and chopped hot peppers in a shallow bowl. Add shrimp and marinate overnight.

Remove shrimp from marinade; dip in remaining olive oil. Thread onto skewers and barbecue over hot coals for about 5 minutes on each side. Serve hot. Serves 6.

Beer Batter Shrimp

⅔ cup flour

⅓ cup corn starch

½ cup water

½ cup beer

1 teaspoon pepper

1 tablespoon oil

1 tablespoon baking powder

1 teaspoon salt

peanut oil for frying

1 pound large shrimp, peeled
but tails left intact

In a medium bowl combine all the ingredients and mix well. Dip shrimp into batter and fry in hot oil until golden brown. Serves 4.

Shrimp Stuffed with Crab

1 pound raw jumbo shrimp,
   shelled and deveined
salt to taste
8 ounces crab meat
2 hard-cooked eggs, finely chopped
2 tablespoons chopped parsley
1 tablespoon finely chopped pimiento
3 slices soft white bread, cubed
2 dashes worcestershire sauce
dash of salt
6 tablespoons melted butter
5 tablespoons mayonnaise, divided
4 teaspoons milk
paprika

Slit each shrimp down the back, slicing deeply to make shrimp lay flat. Salt each shrimp.

Combine crab meat, eggs, parsley, pimiento, bread cubes, worcestershire sauce, salt, butter, and 3 tablespoons mayonnaise. Stuff each shrimp with 1 tablespoon crab meat mixture; place in a buttered baking dish.

Combine remaining 2 tablespoons mayonnaise and milk, stirring well. Pour ½ teaspoon milk mixture over each shrimp; sprinkle with paprika.

Bake at 325 °F for 20 minutes or until stuffing is golden brown and shrimp are pink. Serves 3.

Shrimp Salad

1 pound boiled shrimp
1 cup chopped celery
½ cup mayonnaise
2 tablespoons chopped sweet pickle
salad greens

Drain shrimp. Cover shrimp with ice water and let stand for 5 minutes; drain. Cut large shrimp in half. Combine all ingredients, chill. Serve on salad greens. Serves 6.

Shrimp Tempura

2 small eggs
1 cup milk
1⅛ cups all-purpose flour
½ teaspoon salt
few drops hot sauce
2 teaspoon baking powder
3 pounds large shrimp, peeled
　　but tails left intact
peanut oil for frying

Beat eggs in small mixing bowl, stir in milk. Add flour, salt, and hot sauce; beat until blended. Add baking powder, and mix well. Dip shrimp into batter and fry in hot oil until golden brown, turning once. Drain on absorbent paper. Serve hot. Serves 6.

Spiced Shrimp

2 pounds shrimp
1 bunch celery tops
1 bunch parsley
4 tablespoons mixed pickeling spice
1 cup vinegar
¼ cup salt
2 quarts boiling water

Wash shrimp but do not remove shells. Tie the celery, parsley, and spices in a piece of cheesecloth. Add vinegar, salt, and bag of seasonings to the water. Cover and simmer 45 minutes. Add shrimp, cover, and return to boiling point; simmer 5 minutes. Drain. Serve with cocktail sauce. Serves 6.

Broiled Shrimp

2 pounds raw, peeled, deveined shrimp
3 cloves garlic, minced
½ cup butter melted
2 tablespoons lime juice
½ teaspoon salt
freshly ground pepper
chopped parsley

Cook garlic in butter until tender. Remove from heat. Add lime juice, salt and pepper. Arrange shrimp in a single layer on a baking pan, 15 x 10 x 1 inches. Pour sauce over shrimp. Broil about 4 inches from source of heat for 8 to 10 minutes or until shrimp are pink and tender. Sprinkle with parsley. Serves 6.

Shrimp Cocktail

2 pounds boiled shrimp
½ cup olive oil
1 tablespoon horseradish
1 tablespoon prepared mustard
¼ cup vinegar
1 teaspoon celery seed
½ teaspoon salt
⅛ teaspoon pepper
½ teaspoon onion salt
dash hot pepper sauce

Chill shrimp and place in cocktail cups on cracked ice. Combine other ingredients and serve in small container centered on ice. Serves 6.

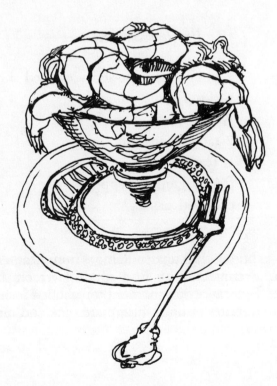

"Boiled" Shrimp

1 pound fresh, raw, unpeeled shrimp
3 cups water
1 teaspoon salt

Add salt to water and bring to boil. Add shrimp and reduce heat. Cover and simmer 3 to 5 minutes, depending on size of shrimp. Drain shrimp and rinse thoroughly under cold running water. Serves 3.

Shrimp Creole

2 pounds unpeeled raw shrimp
1 medium onion, chopped
1 small green pepper, chopped
½ cup sliced celery
½ cup salad oil
2 tablespoons all-purpose flour
1 (16-ounce) can tomatoes
1 (6-ounce) can tomato sauce
2 garlic cloves, chopped
1 bay leaf
1 teaspoon salt
2 teaspoons chili powder
4 dashes hot sauce
1 cup tomato juice
1 can green peas
hot cooked rice

Drop shrimp into boiling salted water to cover; simmer, covered, for 2 to 5 minutes; drain. Peel and devein shrimp; set aside. Saute onion, garlic, green pepper, and celery in hot oil; add flour, and stir until smooth. Add tomatoes, tomato sauce, and seasonings; simmer 15 minutes. Add shrimp and tomato juice; cover and simmer 30 minutes. Add peas to shrimp mixture and cook an additional 10 minutes. Serve over hot cooked rice. Serves 6.

ALPHABETICAL RESTAURANT LISTING

ACKNOWLEDGEMENTS

Tab Tire Repair, Falls Camera, Pica &
Points, Linda S. Brudvig, Susan Santo, Gabe
Fleri, Bob Hammond, Lynne Haas, Dr. Ward
Dorrance, Raymond McAlwee

Whitey Schmidt is author of "The Official
Crab Eater's Guide" and is currently working
on several Chesapeake Bay related books.

Be Picky!

The deliciously savory steamed blue crabs found in the Chesapeake Bay region are among the most sought-after of delicacies for seafood lovers everywhere. Yet even the most dedicated backfin enthusiast has a hard time finding the best crab houses and markets specializing in the fine art of steaming crabs.

This unique year-round guide will provide you with complete details, including maps, on more than 275 of the best eating establishments and seafood markets. Readers will also be treated to delectable crab house recipes as well as the author's own favorites—all seasoned with ample illustrations and poems of praise for the gloriously mouth-watering, sweet, spicy, succulent crab.

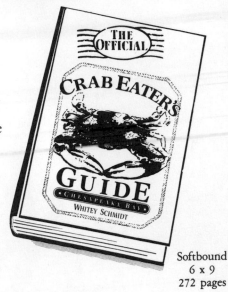

Softbound
6 x 9
272 pages

Please send me _____ copy(ies) of THE OFFICIAL CRAB EATER'S

GUIDE at $8.95 each (plus $1.30 postage and handling—Maryland

residents add$ .45 sales tax). Check enclosed for $ _____

Chesapeake SEAFOOD DINING

A cookbook, a guidebook, a personal pleasure,
a gift to a friend, a wonderful treasure.

Please send me _____ copy(ies) of A GUIDE TO CHESAPEAKE SEAFOOD DINING AT $9.95 each (plus $1.35 postage and handling—Maryland residents add $.50 (sales tax). Check enclosed for $_____

Name _____

Address _____

City _____ State _____ Zip _____

MAIL TO: MARIAN HARTNETT PRESS
Box 51
Friendship Road
Friendship, Maryland 20758